To a lover of class bird
dogs, go my best Wishes.

Al Brenneman

AL BRENNEMAN
TRAINS
BIRD DOGS

AL BRENNEMAN TRAINS BIRD DOGS

By Al Brenneman

THE STRODE PUBLISHERS
HUNTSVILLE, ALABAMA 35801

DEDICATION

I would like to dedicate this book to my wife, Alice, who throughout our married life has permitted me to mix pleasure with business; and to our friend and fellow sportsman Ray Settle who has always been a good sport as well as a friend; and finally I would like to acknowledge the neighborly approach of our next-state-publisher, the Strode Publishing Company of down nearer the Gulf.

Table of Contents

FOREWORD

Over the past several years I have received many requests from all sections of the United States and some foreign countries in regard to my training of the pointing breeds and the retriever breeds. It is not easy in a letter or on the telephone to tell how to train a dog or cure any of the many faults that a dog may have. So I've placed in book form reliable ways to train dogs, and I've called this reliable system the planted bird system.

In this work will be told many of my personal experiences with the dogs I have had in training. The information herein contained is the result of over forty years of work with hunting dogs.

Many years ago when I first started training dogs professionally for the public, I found that I had no set system to train more than six or seven dogs and do a good job. Then when a season came and with it a shortage of birds, I knew that if I wanted to stay in the dog training business I would need some other way to train a paying string of dogs.

My good friend and Hall of Famer Mr. ER. M. Shelley had told me something about his training of hunting dogs by using the common barn pigeon. This interested me greatly because I knew he was training all year long and turning out dogs that were highly trained. He asked me to go to work for him, and of course I jumped at the chance. I soon found that this was the greatest of all ways to really train a class pointing dog and do it in such a short time as compared to the many months of trying to get a dog trained on wild birds. Then, too, this system permits many faults to be cured in dogs that would be hopeless if it were tried with a wild bird system.

It is not easy to forget the past in an era when I worked entirely on wild birds. Some years quail would be plentiful, and you could have a working string of twelve to fifteen dogs. Then would come the dry years when seven or eight covies in a long day's work was all one could find. That is plenty for a day's hunt, but when one makes a living at training dogs, it just isn't enough birds for a paying string of dogs.

By using planted birds and two assistants, I can easily work twenty-five to forty dogs every day and put a far better job of training on each dog and correct faults that would be impossible on wild birds—in general, lessen the time to complete the education of a bird dog.

All bird dogs should have some work afield, commonly called puppy work, for nature to teach them where to search for game. After a few workouts and contact with birds, then the start on the planted birds can begin. However, I have trained many, many dogs that never saw a wild bird until after they were thoroughly trained on planted birds. Those very same dogs that were trained on planted birds before being hunted or worked on wild birds did excellent work in the field. A few hunts on wild birds and nature taught them where to look for wild game. Many dogs that had the proper range for game farm hunting have been hunted their entire life on planted birds.

The question contantly arises among bird dog people as to whether bird dogs can be trained on planted birds as well as wild birds. Some wonder whether or not a dog will make the change over from planted birds to wild birds. Others wonder if a dog will keep interest in planted birds if worked on them for more than a short time. The answer is yes to all of these questions and many more. In fact, it is easier to train on planted birds, and there is less time involved because of the sometimes impossible search for wild birds and the lack of good training grounds.

Training dogs with the use of the planted birds is by no

means a new discovery. Retriever trainers were the first to use them in the development of their dogs for hunting and field trials. They found that by using farm raised ducks, pheasant, or the common barn pigeon in their training they could develop their dogs in the closed season and have them ready for hunting season and ready for field trials too. If you consider that conservation laws in most states will not allow you to take a dog afield from about April 15 until July 15, the dog must lay up in the kennel for three months out of each year. If one is a professional trainer, he has no income for three months. In those three months lost a dog could be trained, and he can legally train on planted birds any time of the year. Even during the open season lack of good hunting grounds to train on or scarcity of game, makes planted bird training important. Even if you have plenty of land to train on, there are work-outs when your dog will not find game and he has learned nothing in the birdless work-out. The time wasted could have been spent in working several dogs on planted birds with complete control over the birds and the dog.

Too many times in work on wild birds the birds may be too jumpy and not hold well while you work your dog, or in curing a birdshy or gunshy where it takes a killed bird to get the job done you just don't have enough birds to kill every day to get the job done. The whole thing about planted bird training is that it is a vehicle to help a dog to point. It teaches him to point staunchly so that you can walk ahead of him to flush the bird to kill it, then stand there until you send him out to find the downed bird and make a prompt and tender retrieve to your hand. It is a vehicle to teach him to honor a bracemate when hunted in pairs or threes, and to hunt where you ask him to quarter the ground. I have used farm raised quail, chukkars, pheasant, and guineas. The cost of each bird is something to think about, so again I recommend the common barn pigeon. All birds mentioned are members of the game bird family except the common barn pigeon. Many people think that a dog will point only game birds, but this isn't true. If worked right, a dog will point any bird used. To repeat, the common barn pigeon is usually plentiful and much cheaper in cost than any of the other birds mentioned.

This is the story of my method of training bird dogs, and the way I cure many faults in dogs that no one else will touch. This is the story of how to properly train dogs with the use of what is termed planted birds. Again, planted birds can be farm raised quail, pheasant, chukkar partridge, guineas, or the common barn pigeon. And again, of all the different birds used, I like the common barn pigeon better than any of the rest. A barn pigeon will lay better, so you can work with your dog on point without flushing if properly dizzied. If you keep a flock of pigeons, and keep them well fed and watered, when flushed they will come up strong in flight, and this is very important to a dog in training. Many would-be trainers, the minute they buy a bunch of pigeons get extremely conservative and want to use the pigeon over and over. So they tie cans, sticks, or ropes on the pigeon so that it cannot fly but a short distance and in so doing spoil what training they have done.

When you use any kind of bird for training, once the dog points it and you have your work completed on the dog, then flush it and kill it. By killing it you can give the dog valuable experience in retrieving. Above all it will develop his desire for birds. You will be surprised how his scenting ability will increase. I have heard many stories over the years of dogs with a poor nose, and usually it was just that the dog had so few birds killed for him he had not really learned to use his nose.

When you kill birds for a dog that has found and pointed them, you are just completing a deal you have made with the dog, and he loves it. Any dog that likes birds can be trained if you use know-how and a lot of common sense.

Pigeons are easy to keep and not hard to get. Fix up a walk-in pen or cage. Make it fifteen or twenty feet long, eight feet wide by six feet tall. Put some poles for roosts across one end and some sort of top over half of it to keep the rain off them. Get a good chicken waterer and a feeder. Feed them shelled corn and furnish them with fine grit, and you are in business.

I have used planted birds to train bird dogs for over thirty-five years, and I still learn from watching the reaction of the dogs in training. You must do it if you are to understand the training of a bird dog. To train dogs, it takes experience, hard work, know-how, and resourcefulness. No two dogs train exactly alike or in the same amount of time. Supported by a certain amount of what might be called "set procedure" or basics, one should be able to try some other approach to any department of training if one method doesn't work.

It is a thrilling sight when you see a good, intelligent, experienced, well-trained dog searching out a field, going to the places that you would go if you were hunting without a dog, pointing, allowing you to flush out the birds for the shot, then on command finding the downed bird and making a prompt and tender retrieve to your hand.

Another thrill to add to it is to say "I trained that dog!"

I believe that anyone who likes to hunt with dogs should train at least one of his own dogs. He will understand much better what goes on in the dog's mind. He will understand why dogs do certain things. He will learn when to correct the dog and when to praise him. He will understand how to recognize the difference between the good dogs with natural ability and those without it. He must study each dog and their reactions to everything done in training.

A bad temper and abuse have no place in training. A little know-how, hard work, and patience are important items in training. Some dogs are like some people; it takes them a little longer to learn. Many trainers expect too much too soon. We must remember that a dog that is starting training doesn't understand one word of our language, so what you are teaching must be done over and over to associate it with a few of the words needed in the education of the dog. You as the trainer must have the know how to get the message across to the student so that he understands.

The methods I use in training are not the results of training one or a dozen dogs, but from the training of hundreds of dogs and studying their reactions. A trainer must be resourceful so that if one method doesn't work he can change to one that will. In the end we want a highly trained dog that is not cowed; we want all the fire, class, and style left in the dog.

You must remember to do a thorough job in every step of training, with reasonable judgement when to punish and when to praise. If you lose your temper, that is a good time to pat the dog gently and then put him in the kennel until the next day when you have cooled off. I have trained many years on wild birds only and many years with the use of planted birds, and when it comes to doing a fine job on a bird dog, whether he is to be used for field trials or just for hunting, I repeat that the best job is by far with the use of planted birds. The whole thing in a nutshell is the control you have over the bird and the student. Faults you can cure with ease on planted birds are: gunshys, birdshys, hard mouth retrievers, blinkers, and dogs that won't mind. All because of your control over the bird used and the student. Any of this work on wild birds would take so long it would be useless.

Every summer hundreds of professional trainers make the trip to Canada or some of the northern states and train on prairie chicken, Hungarian partridge, pheasant, or ruff grouse. These same dogs, when returned to their owners, may be hunted the rest of their hunting days on quail or woodcock but were trained on a different bird. The point is—the dog can be trained on any bird, and if the job is well done the dog will change over to whatever bird he is hunted on. If you can get permission to train on forty or fifty acres of fairly open land, you have enough to train dogs on. You can do it every month of the year unless you live where the snow covers the ground in the wintertime.

CHAPTER I
Choosing Your Bird Dog

If you are new in the dog world and haven't already secured a dog, you may wonder what member of the pointing breed to own as your bird dog. The most popular breeds in the pointing dog group are the English Pointer, English Setter, German Short-Haired Pointer, Irish Setter, and Brittany Spaniel. Any of these breeds are good hunting dogs and with training will point birds.

If you will contact the breeders of the different breeds, you can get a first-hand look at each and something will sell you on one of the breeds over all the others. Beauty is in the eyes of the beholder. The breed that appeals to you may not appeal to others, but it's to be your dog so the choice should be up to you. The important thing is to secure a good prospect that is unspoiled.

Any prospect that I buy I first want to study the pedigree. The dog must be registered or eligible to be registered in the Field Dog Stud book. In that pedigree I want to see the names of dogs that have done considerable winning in field trials. The field trial winning dogs in the pedigree can have done their winning in open or amateur stakes, shooting dog, or open all-age stakes. This gives me the feeling that in this prospect runs the blood of dogs that have proved they were good hunting dogs that could stand the pressure of training and hold it. Then, too, there is a certain amount of pride in a dog with a pedigree of winners in it.

If the pedigree suits, then I'll look at the prospect. Any prospects that I am interested in are usually twelve to twenty months old. I want them old enough to start serious training at once. I have on occasion bought weanling pups, but they were turned loose on the farm and very little was done with them until they were a year old, or more. This gave them time to develop their natural hunting talents.

If you are buying a prospect twelve to twenty months old, there are questions to ask of the seller. How is he with the shotgun? How well started in the field? Is he a head or tail trailer? If you ask how the dog is with a gun, you should ask specifically about the shotgun. Sometimes puppy raisers think they are doing the pups a lot of good by shooting twenty-two caliber shells or blanks near the puppies while they are eating. Puppies can and do become accustomed to the little crack of a twenty-two pistol, but this in my opinion is a foolish waste of time and shells. With a buyer being told that the puppy has been shot over, he then takes the puppy hunting and on contact with game empties a twelve gauge shotgun over the pup and usually has a real gunshy, or one in the making. If you hunt game with a twenty-two or a cap gun, that kind of a start with the gun will no doubt be all right with your dog. Otherwise they should be started in game properly and with the twelve gauge shotgun. This you can do when training your dog on planted birds.

There are some questions in buying a dog that can best be answered when you try the prospect in the field. One thing to watch for is the head trailer or the tail trailer. You won't be happy with either one. In the tryout you will need another dog for a bracemate. The head trailer is usually faster afoot than its bracemate and is more difficult to detect. They never seem to pay any attention to their bracemate but if watched closely will glance in the direction of the bracemate and usually seem to be just a short distance ahead of the mate. The tail-on trailer is easier to detect. It seems that in the thinking of the tail-on trailer this is a race. As youngsters they will yip and bark and practically follow in the footsteps of their bracemate.

There are some dogs that will not hunt in the rain. This of

course can only be discovered by trying them out in the rain. You probably will not expect to hunt in the rain, but if it's a field trial prospect he might get caught in a sudden downpour during his brace, and there goes your entry fee and chance of winning.

In buying a dog, good markings and good conformation are something to look for, but his natural ability is the most important. If he furnishes you with the most game contacts and shooting, you can overlook some poor markings on his coat. In a workout with what the seller calls a started dog you should be able to see what his style is like running and on point even if he only flash points. When he is turned loose for the workout, he should show he is anxious to get started. Some young dogs may yip and bark at the breakaway, but this will wear off soon. He should go to the places that look to you as though there might be birds there. The yearling pup of course will not search out the country as intelligently as a dog that has had three or four years experience, but he should show that he has found game in the right kind of cover before. An older, more experienced dog will

Norwood's King George, 1958-1972, proved to be his owner's wise choice. Norwood's King George was a thirty-five time winner.

probably get on the downwind side of cover for scenting advantage, whereas the yearling may not have figured this out yet.

If the puppy happens to jump a rabbit and gives it chase, it is nothing to worry about. That can be taken care of later. The important thing in looking at a young prospect that is called "started" is to see if he will get out and really go hunting and at least flash point, if only for a few seconds, when he finds birds. This workout provides your best time to see what his range is and whether it will suit your hunting. If you are a foot hunter, then his natural range must be closer than if you hunt from horse or jeep. All dogs will increase their range as they get older and more experienced in searching out the country. The first few minutes of your workout with the young dog may find him running wider than is his natural range. After the edge is worn off, he will show more what to expect of him. Range is what might be called a built-in item. After some dogs become experienced, one dog may do his best job of hunting at one hundred yards while another may do his best at two hundred yards or even a quarter mile. The foot hunter, and especially the grouse and woodcock hunter, must have a dog that is a closer hunter and one that checks in now and then.

If you have decided on the breed you want, then you must decide on whether it should be male or female. As far as training is concerned, one will take training as well as the other. An important thought concerns the kenneling together of a male and female or the kenneling together of two males. If it's a male and female together, then twice a year the female will come into season and if not kenneled alone each time for about twenty-seven days, you could end up with a litter of puppies. One thing you can do is to have the female spayed. For myself I do not recommend this because too many times the female that is spayed becomes fat and keeps getting fatter all the time. If it's two males, they may get along for a short time, then possibly when no one is around a fight breaks out and usually the owner ends up with one dead dog or a crippled one. The safest way all around is to have two runs with separate dog houses. It is important to have good kenneling arrangements: plenty of shade for the hot weather including a good insulated kennel for coolness in the summer and warmth in the winter. A chain link fence with a top on it will stop a lot of worries about a dog escaping. All dogs should be vaccinated, and owners should have their dogs examined by a veterinarian for heart worms and stomach worms.

Chapter II
TRAINING EQUIPMENT NEEDED

It doesn't take a long list of items to train a dog, but the equipment should be the best. You should have heavy, well-made collars that fit the dog properly. Dogs in training become excited when they see the other dogs working and can break the cheap leather collars. Nylon collars are very good. The collar should fit so that you can slide your finger between the collar and the dog's neck. A collar too loose can let a dog slide out of it at a time when you may be working with another dog. A collar too tight of course will shut off a dog's breathing naturally.

Put a one-and-one-half-inch harness ring to snap the leash or checkline to. It will save a lot of wear and tear on a collar if it is not riveted or sewed to the collar. If it is a leather collar, treat the collar with olive oil occasionally, but let it dry thoroughly before putting it on the dog's neck so it will not blister. You will need a whistle. The large black hard-rubber or plastic referee's whistle is the best. In cold weather it will not freeze to your lips.

You will need a shotgun for your training. For this I buy a good single barrel twelve gauge gun. They are not expensive and will last usually until eight or ten cases of shells have been shot through them. You can drop them on the ground, and you don't have to worry as you would with a high priced gun. It also has a safety feature. Once it has been fired while working with a dog it is harmless if you dropped it and accidentally step on it or because an inexperienced helper is handling it. After having too many shotguns pointed at me, I have become permanently gunshy without hope of cure. Most guns of this grade come as full choke guns. Saw off about four inches of the barrel, and it's just right for a training gun.

To force train your dog to retrieve, you will need what is known as a retrieving buck. Actually you will need two bucks. One with legs and one without legs. These bucks can be made out of an old hoe handle or shovel handle. Usually these handles are made out of oak or hickory and are hard enough to discourage a dog to some extent from biting down or being hard-mouth. To make them, saw them eight inches long. One will be all right just as it is. The other should have two holes drilled in each end so that you can put large nails through each end. Then the buck will stand off the floor about two inches. During the force retrieving training, both bucks will come into use.

If you plan on training more than one dog, make a feed or stake-out chain. This chain should be made out of fairly heavy chain because dogs jumping and pulling can break a lightweight

To force train your dog to retrieve, you will need two retrieving bucks, one with legs, and one without.

19

chain. I use a water-well chain forty or forty-five feet long. On each end I put a heavy two-and-a-half-inch ring using large cold-shuts to fasten it to the chain. In the field I can drive an old car axle through the rings about two feet and feel sure the dogs will not pull the chain loose while I am working with a dog in the field. Starting about eighteen inches from the ring on one end I use a lighter weight piece of chain about fifteen inches long fastened to the heavy chain with a cold-shut that can be riveted shut. On the other end of the light weight chain I use a brass swivel harness snap. Now you have a place on the chain for one dog. Now prepare another fifteen-inch chain with swivel snap. The best way is to put a dog on the first chain, then with the new chain snap it on the second dog's collar. Then using an open cold-shut, attach it to the heavy chain to see whether either dog can reach the other. Usually four to five feet is not too much. When working dogs in the field, the dogs left on the chain become excited and will grab at each other and can hurt each other so watch the spacing closely. The dogs on the long chain can learn a great deal from watching those working in the field. One of the most important items in dog training is the checkline. It will give you all the advantage needed in teaching a dog to obey you, and if he doesn't obey you at all times he is not a trained dog. Without the checkline you cannot train a dog properly. It is good to keep several checklines on hand at all times. Sometimes one may get broken or a dog may chew one in two, so as with all equipment a spare or repair part is advisable.

It takes a good bit of practice and work to be clever and efficient with a checkline. A mistake with it can possibly hurt you or unnerve a young dog in training so that he is set back in his training. The checkline is used in dog training for control over the dog so that he cannot get up too close to planted birds or jump in to try to flush them after he has pointed them. The checkline keeps him close to you and enables you to bring him to you when the time comes. With it you can teach him to come when called and to quarter the ground ahead of you.

When the time comes to steady your dog for the shot at the kill, your checkline will play a most important part. You must

If you plan on training more than one dog, make a feed or stake-out chain.

learn to play the checkline in and out as needed when getting close to where a bird is planted. If you don't take up the slack in the line as needed, your dog could get to the bird and flush it or catch it. Sometimes a young dog lacking experience will not use his nose as much as an older or more experienced dog, and you must let him swing past where the bird is planted two or three times to help him get the scent of the planted bird. Thus the checkline must be at the right length so he can't run over the bird before he gets scent and so that he is not jerked too hard to scare him or cow him. The handler must also be careful that he doesn't have some of the line tangled around his own feet or legs. If the handler lets loose of the line for some reason and it is around his feet or legs, he can get a bad fall. A running fifty-or-sixty-pound dog has a lot of power. For regular field work a number-nine-or-ten-size nylon checkline is the best, forty feet long. On the end is fastened a non-swivel harness snap. Also have on hand a line twenty feet long and probably one or two ten-foot ones.

You will need what is called a flushing whip. They are seldom used for flushing birds but to punish a dog for a wrong doing. They are an important part of the training equipment and must be used very carefully and with good judgment.

Sometimes you may be training where there is no stream to water the dogs so add to your equipment a five gallon cream can and wash pan to water each dog before and after his workout. A small wire crate to carry a few birds should about complete your training equipment needs.

CHAPTER III
Working The Young Dog In The Field
or
Dogs Too Young For Serious Training

If you have secured a weanling puppy, there isn't much you can do with it in regard to serious training until it is eleven or twelve months old or, even better, fifteen to eighteen months old. It would be a good thing if a person had two puppies of this age to raise. It would cut down on the lonesomeness of a puppy if it had a playmate and probably leads to less crying and barking at night. Then, too, your odds are doubled that you will get at least one good one. I believe there is something lacking in puppies that are raised and kenneled alone.

First, have your veterinarian check the puppies for worms. Then the complete vaccination deal: distemper, rabies and parvo. It's cheap health insurance.

Without a doubt the best way to raise puppies is to let them run loose on a farm where they can get acquainted with all the farm animals. Puppies raised around farm animals get used to animals and poultry and later when being hunted do not bother them if they run across them in the field. I have had puppies in training that were farm-raised where the farm had goats among the farm animals. These dogs did not bother deer when hunted in deer country. There is always the possibility that a young dog may want to bother livestock or poultry. When this occurs one should start with a little punishment and teach the word "No". This is a one-word command that can come into use all of the dog's life. When the puppy or young dog bothers stock or poultry or anything that is not wanted, get to the dog and give him a shaking by the collar and repeat the word "No" several times as you shake him. As soon as this word is instilled into the dog's memory and he knows that it is a command and that he will be punished if he continues to do a thing, even if he is a good distance from you he will mind. This command can be useful when you are hunting and the dog is going off in the wrong direction.

If you call out "No" a time or two, you will notice that he will go to the front, or the direction you go. When a trainer needs to punish a young dog or puppy, the trainer should keep in mind that the animal shouldn't be punished too severely. It is not how much punishment is given but the way it is given and the command that is given with it. If he continues to do something not wanted, then you must increase the punishment a little. After each instance of punishment, hold the dog a minute or two, and talk to him and pet him a little. With any dog there is always the possibility of too much whipping that causes the dog to be shy and cowed. Never call a dog to you to punish him. Go to him and catch him. After you call a dog to you a few times and then punish him he will soon get to where he will not come. That is a part of canine reasoning power.

Having your dog drag a check-cord gives you a certain amount of advantage in catching the dog for correction. You can use a shorter light-weight line for younger dogs and a heavier one for the older mature dogs. Young dogs that are farm raised will do some self hunting, and mother nature will teach them many good things. They will mature sooner than puppies that are left in a kennel the early part of their lives. If permitted to run loose too long, young dogs can pick up bad habits that are hard to break. When pups reach the age of six to eight months, it is time to put them in the kennel so that from then on you can supervise their workouts. Dogs that run loose all their lives never seem to have the fire and dash one likes in a good classy bird dog. If they do run loose all the time, there just isn't the thrill for them. Dogs that are hunted too long hours too

24

many days are not too thrilling to watch.

If you cannot have your pup grow up in the country, then he must be kenneled and you should try to get him out as often as possible. If he is a very young puppy, take him to meadows where the going is not too tough.

One should keep in mind that a young puppy is not strong enough for long workouts. If the puppy is six months to a year old, his muscles haven't developed enough to carry him for long periods of time. Fifteen or twenty minutes for a workout is long enough until he has matured some and built up his stamina. As he becomes older and stronger, then you can increase the length of time for his workouts. Try to work him in the country where he has a good chance of finding game shortly after he has been turned loose for his workout. Shortly after he has found game and had a good chase is a good time to pick him up and call it a workout. He will remember this contact with game the next time you take him afield and will show it in his desire to start hunting. The oftener you can give him these short workouts the better. Very soon you will see the advancement in his knowledge of where to look for game. You will notice that he will not run back to you or jump upon you. He will stay busy with his hunting. Don't wear him out in these workouts.

Puppies sometimes start the habit of running back to you every now and then. They are wasting time, and while the dog is fairly young is the time to teach him to stay out at work until you call him in. When the dog starts back to you, give a short blast on your whistle and at the same time run at your dog as though to drive him out, no matter what direction, just so that you cause him to go out. The first few times you may not see much improvement, but like every bit of training it must be done over and over to get results. It may be well to carry a small bush and as you start at your dog to shake it at him. It may scare him a little at first, but if you use reason here and not overuse the bush you will soon see that even just a short blast on the whistle when you start towards him will send him out. There are some dogs that never figure this out, but they are rare if the training is carried out properly.

One mistake that many owners make is to take a puppy to start in the field and at the same time to take along either the mother or an older dog that has had experience. The usual result after several workouts is that you have made a trailer out of the puppy. The puppy is not strong enough or fast enough to furnish much of a race, so he spends his time just trying to keep up with the older dog. Then when the older and more experienced dog finds game, the puppy is right there. The contact with the game is good, but the puppy then thinks in order to get in on this fun he must stay close to the dog that found the game, and that's where the trailer has his first and lasting lesson. If this type of workout is continued, the puppy becomes a confirmed trailer and always dependent on his bracemate to find game.

Puppies that have been brought to me for training that have had that kind of start in the field would hardly hunt when turned loose alone. They kept looking for the bracemate, and it took a good bit of extra work to cure this fault. It's a very hard fault to cure and in some well developed cases is never completely cured. The approach to a cure is to work the dog many, many times alone and into lots of birds. This can be done by using pigeons and killing one for the dog every workout. One must remember that faults are always acquired through an accident or improper handling. With the proper care and work in handling, most dogs can be restored. After your dog seems to be very interested in finding game on his own, you can then try him with a bracemate. This bracemate should be a slow and close working dog. The young dog may not now be satisfied to stay in close. It is much easier to avoid making a trailer than curing one.

If you want to widen your dog's range some, work him in as open a type of prairie country as you can. Whether you are on foot or on a horse you yourself stay a little farther away from promising looking cover, such as thickets and fence rows. Your puppy will see this cover and go to it.

To teach your puppy his name, use it often. He can hear a short sharp name more plainly and will remember it best. When you feed him, use his name several times. When you pet and make over him, use his name. Little by little if his name has been used when things are good for him, and to him, you will notice that he responds to it. If he doesn't, when he is a little older and the serious training starts, force can be used in teaching his name.

One of the "Don'ts" about puppies involves development of sight pointing. All of us like to see what the puppy will look like on point. To develop this, trainers tie a quail wing to one end of a string and then tie the other end to a fishpole. With a little time spent with the puppy, the puppy will point the wing. But as with everything, this can easily be overdone. The puppy soon learns to sight-point everything he sees until it becomes a nuisance. Even though he sight-points staunchly, he isn't learning anything. To point wild birds, he has to use his nose to point them because he will not be able to see many wild birds in time to get them pointed. The thinking here is to leave sight pointing out of the training program. It has absolutely nothing to offer in the good of dog training.

The dog should, of course, be taught to be staunch under all circumstances. Sometimes in trials where game farm birds are released a bird may leave his cover and walk out in front of the pointing dog, and if he hasn't been taught to be staunch you have just been counted out in the stake. This training should come when the dog is in the serious part of the training.

CHAPTER IV
Introduction Of The Shotgun

If a puppy has reached the age of ten or twelve months, he is old enough to be introduced to the shotgun. Previous to this age, one had better leave the gun out of the picture for a while. Great care must be taken in this part of training no matter what age the dog is. As mentioned previously, the best gun for training any hunting dog is the twelve gauge single shotgun. One shot is enough at this stage of the work, and if you throw the gun on the ground to do some work with the dog it won't go off should you step on it.

The use of the twenty-two or thirty-two calibre does nothing for a puppy, and they do not sound like a shotgun. There have been far too many dogs made gunshy by the use of the twenty-two and thirty-two. These weapons are recommended erroneously by the so-called experts who write about gunshys but have never cured the first dog yet. If you start your dog the correct way and do it with a shotgun, you won't need the small bore gun. To start the young dog with the shotgun, leave the gun at home. The dog will tell you when to bring the gun, as he will tell you when to move up to the next step of any part of his training. There are two areas to train a dog with a shotgun. One is to take the dog to a field to look for wild birds. The other is to use planted birds. Let's start with the wild birds.

To use wild birds to introduce your dog to a shotgun, every day or two at first without your shotgun take your dog to the field where you feel he will find game. Sometimes a puppy may be a little frightened when he finds his first birds. Should he show signs of being the least bit afraid, do not pet him or talk to him, but just continue hunting and try to find the singles out of that covey. He will probably run over them, and if only one or two get up he may then give chase. Keep this work up time after time until he is breaking out and chasing every bird that gets up. Three or four times into birds is not enough. Maybe fifteen or twenty times isn't enough. One can't say until the puppy shows that he knows what he is hunting and really puts them in the air and goes after them. Should he start a rabbit, let him chase it and do not scold him. The more he chases no matter what, the better you are preparing him for the gun. The trouble with too many people is that we get in a hurry and if a dog makes one or two good chases we're tempted to shoot the gun.

When the young dog has been taken to the field enough times and into game enough, he will tell you when you arrive at the field and let you know that he wants to get started to go hunting. When he is showing this and you feel that he has been into plenty of game, then take your single barrel twelve gauge shotgun along. This may be the big day. If he runs over a covey or chases a rabbit or pheasant, count three and pull the trigger. Don't wait too long but see that he is in full chase. He probably will not hear the gun.

A word of warning. Some young dogs may by now be using their nose enough to point birds. Should this happen to your dog, walk in and flush the birds but do not shoot unless he breaks quickly to chase. If he breaks quickly, and continues his chase, then shoot your shotgun once. Keep this work up for a few more workouts. Then you may try shooting twice quickly. If he is o.k., now you may consider him nicely started with the shotgun.

If he doesn't chase be very careful; there may be a timid streak in the dog. At the least he is warning you that he is not ready. One must not be in a hurry in this stage of training. A mistake here can really set you back in hard work.

If the dog should quit chasing when the gun is fired and

come in to you, do not pet him or try to soothe him in any way. Just keep on trying to find more birds. Should more birds be found do not shoot, for your dog has just told you he is not ready.

Now for our second way to introduce a dog to a shotgun, an introduction with planted birds. This is the easier way, especially if you live where you cannot have enough land to run on or where birds are too scarce or out of season. To begin with you should obtain three or four dozen pigeons and have them in your pigeon holding pen for use as you need them. Never run out of pigeons or it will set your training work back, and don't be stingy with them. Quail could be used, but pigeons are less costly and easier to handle and lay for the dog's work.

For this work you should have a helper. Give the helper full instructions before you start so that he will know exactly what he is to do without having to improvise his own steps. You and he will both need to know how to dizzy a pigeon. In your pigeon holding pen is the best place to learn this and practice it. You won't lose any pigeons in the pen.

Take a good strong pigeon in your right hand with your thumb against the bird's left wing and your fingers against his right wing. Now rotate the bird quickly as though you were cranking a car. If the bird has been well fed on cracked corn or shelled corn, you will see the feed start to come out of his mouth. He is then sick and dizzy and will not try to fly in this condition. Now gently pull his head around under either wing. Lay him on the ground and let your hand rest on him a few seconds and you will note that he will lay there for several minutes before he is able to fly. Take note of this because when you dizzy a pigeon to be used in training you should have some idea how long he will lay. When dizzying in the field for training, lay the pigeon on the side with the head down.

On using quail: if one is going to use quail to train on, then he should build what we call a recall pen, or cage. This cage should be four feet long by two feet wide by two feet high. There should be a partition to separate the cage part from the room which is a shelter for the quail from rain. This should be

If you practice dizzying a pigeon in its pen, you will know how long to expect the pigeon to lay still when you begin serious training in the field.

covered with plywood. The birds will go into this room if dogs or animals bother around the quail pen. The floor part of this cage should be covered with one-half-inch mesh wire. Their droppings will drop through this, and the birds will be fairly sanitary. On one side of the cage a funnel should be made out of half-inch mesh wire for the quail to walk back into the quail holding pen. Twenty is about the right number of birds to put into this, and fed and watered, they will soon call this home. Usually in twenty days they can be depended upon to come back regularly. Except that around the middle of March or the first of April these birds normally will not return to the recall cage. It is then the mating season. These birds will mate and will raise real top grade young birds that will furnish you with a new wild covey of quail.

To train caged birds to come back, do not bother such birds for about three weeks. Then open the door and let five or six out and gently close the door and get away from the cage.

Try not to flush them. They will start to work at going through the funnel to get back in with the other birds. Do this four or five days. Then they can be taken about one hundred yards from the cage and used in dog training after which they will return to their home, the cage.

You should have a small carrying cage about twenty inches long and about the size of the quail service door. Put this cage at the door and drive the quail (usually six or seven) into it. In this carrying cage you can carry the quail to where you plan to do any dog training.

There, the helper must dizzy the pigeon and put it in the grass, which should be ten to twelve inches high to help hide the bird. Sprinkle grass lightly over the bird to cover it. Not too much or it will not get up good to fly. The helper should use a small limb or bush to mark the exact spot so the handler will know just how close he can come to the planted bird.

While the helper is preparing the bird, the handler will put a forty foot checkline on the dog's collar and let him cast about to do some hunting. Work in somewhat of a circle, using in time six or eight minutes, then work toward where the helper placed the pigeon and and marker. By this time the helper himself has returned to the truck so he will not cause the dog to be interested in him instead of hunting. Now you must work your dog toward the planted bird, but you should use caution that the wind is to your back so that the dog cannot scent the bird. This all must come as a surprise to him. As you get within a few feet of the planted bird, stop, and by now the helper has come out to where you are with the dog.

Your helper now will try to get the dog's attention by kicking around some in the grass. He must not flush the bird yet but must get the attention of the dog. The handler has come up fairly close to the dog and has worked his way up on the checkline so that the dog has but ten or twelve feet of line. When you have the dog's attention, the helper will roll out the pigeon to make it fly. If it doesn't fly at once, don't let the dog grab it. When the bird does flush to fly, drop the checkline and let the dog chase. Be careful that you are not standing on the checkline because this might shock the dog or hurt you. This workout should be repeated daily in the same manner. To say how many times, you can't.

The dog will tell you when to use the gun. To use twelve or fifteen pigeons before using the shotgun is a bargain. When the dog is showing plenty of boldness in this work, then have the helper take the shotgun to where the pigeon will be flushed. When the dog breaks out to chase, the helper will shoot and kill the pigeon. Then day after day kill one pigeon for the dog. Let the dog do whatever he wants to with the dead bird. After several days of this kind of work have the helper use a double barrel and fire the second shot after the first shot kills the bird.

This work has all been done to create interest and excitement in the dog for the bird so that you can shoot and not have a dog that is gunshy or afraid of the flush of birds. This work has been done without working the dog upwind from where he could smell the bird. Surprise to the dog is the reasoning here. As he retrieves and plays with the dead bird the dog learns what a bird smells like. When the serious part of training comes, then the dog will be worked upwind and allowed to smell the birds as he hunts. The surprise to him will almost guarantee that he will point planted birds with a stiff tail.

CHAPTER V
Obedience Training (Yard Training)

Up to now the work with your pup has been in letting him grow up into a mature dog. You have taught him his name, and gotten him started in the field hunting so that he knows where to look for game. If the training so far has been done well and he is a year old or more, he is ready for more serious training. Training so far has been to build your pup into a bold and fearless dog that has but one thing on his mind and that is to hunt and find birds, flush them, and give them a chase in the hope he can catch them. Yet even though he has matured to this point he still is not the type of dog that will enable you to get many shots at game. So the training from now on should emphasize the bringing of your dog under control. He should be able to point birds so that you can walk, not run to him. You should be able to flush birds so that you can shoot a bird and still have your dog stand there until you send him out to make a prompt tender retrieve to your hand. If he is hunted with a bracemate, then he must know that he is to stop at a reasonable distance when he sees another dog on point, and stay there until sent on hunting.

A dog without even the yard training initial phase of obedience training is more of a nuisance than a credit. There are many things involved in a dog's obedience, not incidently just a hunting dog's but any kind of dog's. Many times people have come to me after seeing one of my dogs in training or at a field trial and have asked how I can make them perform so perfectly.

The answer to such questions is that they are put through their training work day after day until they do it perfectly. Even after they are what we call "trained" they still go through their work daily. They may of course be allowed to go without work a few days now and then, but to have them sharp and show-worthy calls for day after day work. This makes them perform perfect-ly. The dog himself will tell you when you can let up a little on his obedience training.

The work so far has been on early development of dog training. The dog has been taught to properly search out the country ahead of him. After he found birds in the right places a few times, he learned that if he goes to what we call likely-looking places he may find game. His natural instincts are to point when he scents game, when backing a bracemate, or when pick-ing up a bird that has been shot or a bird simply caught by the dog himself. The "point" is nothing more than the "pause" before the leap. Many animals point. The point or pause that an animal makes just before the leap is made because the animal's nose is trying to get the scent just right. He wants to pinpoint where the game is so that when he makes the leap he will be accurate in pouncing upon the game wherever it may be. Man has added to this pointing instinct in the bird dog by train-ing him to be "staunch" on point. This means that the dog is not to flush the birds by leaping toward them before the gunner is close enough to get a good shot. More refinement has been added to this polish by teaching the dog to stop in his tracks when he sees another dog on point.

Another step in the refinement is to teach the dog to gently pick up the bird and deliver it to the hunter promptly instead of following a natural instinct to take the bird and bury it for later use as food. The final step in refinement is to teach the dog to stand after the flush and shot until sent out to make the retrieve, or until sent on hunting.

A dog must be steady to shot and wing if successful in the greatest of all sports, bird dog field trials. Even as a youngster I learned the value of a dog steady to shot. My teacher was an English setter, as good a teacher as any one could have for hunting birds. But his anxiousness to retrieve the one bird I might kill with my single shotgun would many times cause him to run over a sleeper that didn't flush with the bevy, and that sleeper would get away and the dollar I was getting for the bird went too. After I taught the dog to stand there until I could reload my gun, I was able to get shots that I had been unable to do before.

In order to teach any of these refinements it is absolutely necessary that the dog be given an intense yard training course. All dogs need this training whether they are members of the non-sporting group or are one of our hunting companions. Obedience is the foundation of all training. In bird dogs there are four commands that are really needed. They are: heel—whoa—come—and fetch. Other commands may be taught as needed. The most important of these commands is the word "whoa." With this command you have the key to complete control. If your dog becomes confused in and around game, if he is close to another dog that is pointing and does not see him, or even if he starts across a road where there may be traffic, if that one word "whoa" is well trained in him it can be an all-important command. Absence of that command is like driving your car without brakes.

"Heel" taught well will change your dog from a pulling, tugging horse to a gentlemanly companion that will walk with you through the field or down the street without the nuisance aspects of an untrained dog. The third important command is "come." Your dog should learn to come promptly and happily when the command "come" is given.

There are other commands that some obedience trainers teach. Two that are an absolute "no" for bird dogs are "sit" or "lie down." These are all right for other breeds and a "must" for dogs in the bench shows in their obedience classes, but not in class bird dogs.

As in all parts of training there is a proper time for the yard or obedience training to be given. To give this training too early in the dog's life means that it may be more difficult to teach some of the other very important things such as staunchness on point. The best time for the obedience course is after the dog is well started in the field and has found birds many times and is as bold as a lion in his work.

If it is taught well, a young dog will remember the first things taught him better than anything else learned throughout his life, for this reason the young dog should be given his introduction to the field and birds first. I have had young dogs sent to me for training that had been given a thorough course in obedience training before they had been worked in the field to develop their hunting instinct. Each and every one of them wanted to walk with me at heel, and it took a great deal of extra time to break this training so they would get out and hunt. Even then some of them would stop hunting and drop in at heel. Then when we would come to the part of training where the young dog is to be taught to honor a bracemate's point, he would become nervous and either sit down or drop to his belly.

The young dog on his first few points is sometimes a little nervous, and using the checkline too roughly to keep him from jumping in to flush birds may unduly make him unsettled.

Sitting or dropping on point is usually very hard to break and may show up many times later in life, especially on occasions when the dog is working some spooky or jumpy birds. There are dogs that will drop on point that have had little or no yard or obedience training. They are usually the cautious or false pointing dogs that may have been handled too roughly in staunching them on point. If the young prospect has had the proper start in the field on wild game, the chances are very good that he will not sit or lie down on point.

When I feel the dog is ready, I start the yard training of "heel," "whoa," and "come." Any of the steps in a dog's training should be started where there is nothing to distract his attention. You must have his complete and undivided attention one hundred percent. After your dog has been worked several times and you feel he knows and understands what you are trying to do, then you can work him where there are some things to distract him. This is the time to force him to give you his complete attention and obey the commands that you give him. As

When yard training your dog to "heel," make things easier by walking your dog next to a long-building or a fence. Keep the dog between you and the building or the fence.

his training progresses he will learn that he must give you his attention and obey regardless of what is happening around him, or there will be some punishment.

The first thing I teach in yard training is for the dog to "heel" on my left side. I want him to "heel" at whatever speed I walk and to be alert should I make a quick turn to the right or left. Use your twenty foot checkline and snap it to your dog's collar. You will need a whip for this work. Put the dog on your · left side with the checkline in your left hand, the whip in your right. The dog will try to run forward, pull backward, and to both sides when this work is first started. To make things a little easier take him to a long building or next to a fence with the dog between you and the building or fence. Start walking forward with the checkline up fairly short so that he doesn't have much running or pulling room. As you start give the command "heel" several times so that he will soon get used to the word. As he starts to make the run forward, jerk him back sharply and

38

if he persists strike him with the whip across the chest, meanwhile repeating the command "heel." Should he try to lag back, jerk sharply to bring him up. Good sharp jerks will get his attention. Should he duck behind you and over to your right side, snap the whip across his nose and bring him back to your left side. With the building on your left you shouldn't have much trouble there. By using the command every time you correct him, you soon will get him to understand that he is to walk with you with his head about even with your left leg. After a few days he should be heeling so that he only needs an occasional correction. Of course when needed, be alert and quick to correct him.

After a few days you can take him away from the fence or building because by now he should be doing fairly well on the heeling. If he wants to pull away to your left, sharp jerks to bring him up beside you should be given. If he still wants to pull out to the left, put the checkline in your right hand and the whip in your left and hold it to the dog's left side. When he pulls out slap him on the side with the whip, giving the command "heel." When he begins to show you that he knows what you are teaching and is working fairly well, walk at different speeds and make right and left turns. This will cause him to be more alert. The more often you can give these lessons the sharper he will be in his work. Two or three times a day is better than once a day, but the lessons should not be over ten or fifteen minutes. A lesson too long makes a dog listless and, like, you, makes him tired of the work. If properly done without abuse to the dog but with proper correction, he will look forward happily to his lesson and his being with you.

As your lessons continue, give the checkline some slack always so the dog will not expect to do his work on a tight checkline. After you get the "feel" that your dog will obey you, then you can drop the checkline and try him to see whether he will walk at heel. Should he try to dart away you can quickly step on the line and pick it up to give him several hard jerks to let him know that you will punish him if he doesn't obey. If your dog should break away from you and make a run for the kennel, go after him quickly and give him three or four sharp licks with the whip, then jerk him back to where you were working him. Give him a few more minutes work now even though you were about to quit training at the time he broke away. Never quit training on a poor performance. One must be alert and quick to correct a dog when he disobeys. If you correct him promptly, the dog will know why you are punishing him. Always at the end of the workout spend a few minutes making over the dog. He will look forward to working for you each day.

If you plan on running your dog in field trials or working him from a horse, you should teach him to walk or trot along beside a horse at the command of "heel." For dogs that have not been around livestock, the dog will need to be around the horse until he is not afraid of it or doesn't want to play with it or jump up on it. Usually long enough is a day or two of leading your dog around the horse, letting him smell it and just being around it. The horse that you use for this lesson should be an extremely gentle horse and one that will not kick or be excitable. You must be sure that the horse will not hurt or scare the dog.

To start out, have your dog at "heel" on your left side and your horse on your right, holding the reins to lead the horse with. Give the command to "heel" to the dog and start walking in large circles and making turns to the right and left. If your dog shows signs of any shyness of the horse, stop a moment and let the dog smell around the horse and then start again with the "heel" command. If he shows no signs of worry about the horse, you can then mount your horse and give the "heel" command. Give the dog enough lead rope so that it is not tight or pulling on him. If he pulls off to the front, side, or back, give him a sharp jerk to bring him alongside your horse. Any time you correct him give the "heel" command. You must watch closely that your dog doesn't run around back of the horse and get the rope around the horse's hind legs or you may dismount from your horse in an unorthodox way. The oftener you can give this work the quicker your dog will learn to walk at "heel"

If you plan on running your dog in field trials or working him from a horse, you should teach him to walk or trot along beside a horse at the command of "heel."

by your horse. He will learn to do so as well as he does when you are walking with him.

After your dog is well trained at "heeling," then it is time to teach "whoa," the most important command he will ever learn. Because "whoa," is the important command that it is, great care must be taken that it be taught correctly. Once the dog has learned it he will never forget it. For this part of the training the first few days he should be taken to a place where there are no distractions, such as other dogs or people. Dogs in training are always anxious to give their attention to anything else. You must have their complete attention if you are to do a good job of training in a reasonable time. Out behind the barn or in a large room in a building will be good.

If it's some place the dog has never been, give him a little time to look the place over to put his mind at ease. As soon as he seems to be satisfied in his surroundings, start out by heeling him around a little to get his mind on training and to know he is here to obey commands.

After you have been heeling a few moments, stop and say "whoa." Naturally he will not understand the new command nor will he obey, but when used several times he will. While you have stopped, put the lead in your right hand and with your left hand stroke the dog's back gently but firmly and repeat the new command "whoa" several times. He won't obey this at this time, but it's a start in letting him hear the word. Now take the lead and heel him around the room and repeat the "whoa" procedure several times. Fifteen minutes is long enough for the lesson. If you can do it again this day, so much the better.

After three or four days, you can be more firm in teaching this command. The trainer will need the whip and good common sense in the use of it. One important thing in the training of a dog is that the dog should know what the whip is but not be afraid of it. If your whip has a wristlet on it, wear it while you are around the dog so that he will become accustomed to seeing it. Use the whip at times to rub him around the head and back. From your training him in heeling he should have learned something of the whip that you carry. He should have learned that it will not hurt him unless he does not obey a command.

After you have worked the dog at "heel," stop and say "whoa." Hold your checkline in your left hand and your whip in your right hand. Take a step back, as the dog starts to follow, then strike him lightly across the chest and give the command "whoa" again. This will startle him for moment, and he may start to you again, in which case you must tap him again across the chest and give the command "whoa." Don't let him stand but a few seconds the first few times. Then step up to him and stroke him on the back repeating the command "whoa," after which heel him a little bit and then give him the command "whoa" again. Don't expect too much the first two or three days. Then when you see he is starting to stand for you to step back, then try another step or two. If he comes to you or even starts, quickly take him by the collar and take him back to where he was and repeat the "whoa" procedure. In a very few days he will be standing at "whoa" for you to walk around him. To make him even tighter at "whoa," as you are standing

Take great care and teach the command "whoa" correctly; it is the most important command the dog will ever learn.

facing him, gently pull on the checkline. If this causes him to start to you, strike the checkline sharply and say "whoa." With a little practice you can make the dog brace himself against you pulling on the line.

All during any part of yard training, stop a moment or two and make over the dog. Then go back to training. After a week's work with him, you should have him standing while you walk circles around him or walk off twenty feet or so, or whatever the length of the checkline you are using.

You can by now use the forty foot checkline and work up the distance a few feet farther each day. If you do your training every day, your dog will gain in his training quickly. Now is the time to start teaching the command "come." At the same time if the dog doesn't seem to know his name very well it is a good time to teach it with force and kindness. As you have him standing at "whoa," have hold of the end of the checkline and say "come" and use his name and give a quick and sharp jerk to you. If he comes to you, make over him greatly. If he doesn't come on to you, jerk him to you with the rope and each time you jerk say "come" (name). Any time he doesn't come quickly jerk on the rope and call his name. Some dogs are a little hard to teach the "come" command. If so take hold of the rope about a foot from his collar and give several sharp jerks, meanwhile using the command and his name. In a few days he will almost jump at you when the command is given.

If he is doing a good job of "whoa" at forty feet and coming when you call him, then put him at "whoa" at forty feet and walk off a short distance and call him to you. When he gets about halfway to you speak the command "whoa" sharply. If he doesn't stop on the command, go to him and take him back to where he should have stopped. When you have "whoa" well taught in the yard, try him in the field where he may be more difficult to control. You will have the forty foot checkline on his collar which will give you an advantage in getting to him quickly if he doesn't stop when you give the command. Let him cast around hunting a few minutes before giving the command to "whoa." Then as he casts past you give the command and be ready to make a run for the checkline. If he doesn't stop promptly, catch him and take him back to the spot where he should have stopped and scold him and then make him stand at "whoa" for a minute or two. Then it is back to training, over and over.

Always remember you must never give a command in training that you can't get to your dog to enforce. Dogs soon learn to obey if you can get to them and not to obey if they are where you can't get to them. Try and give this lesson as often as possible, but do not make the workouts too long. Always remember that when he does a command right, reward him with praise and petting. This is force training, but don't cow him or make him dislike the training or you with abuse. If done properly your student will be bold and happy in all parts of his work.

One should never completely discontinue yard training. It is the key to your control over your dog. If you do not have control over your dog, he will not be very useful to you. After he is well trained in yard work, it can then be done every few days just to keep him sharp. With your dog well yard trained, then use the training whenever you take him out for a workout in the field. Make him "heel" from the kennel to the car. "Heel" him from the car to the starting place in the field. Then make him "whoa" before being told "all right" to start hunting. Go through the commands when you take him back to the kennel. Always have the checkline so that you can enforce your commands, and be sure to use his name as often as possible.

In the training of a dog, a command that is valuable and useful is the word "no." You will need it and use it many times. It will surprise you how well a dog can tell the difference between the words "no" and "whoa" even at considerable distance.

Usually a young dog when taken to the field is very anxious to be turned loose to hunt. This is good and he should be. It's a good sign in a dog of any age. As the trainer you are teaching control over the dog, and here is a good time to put a little extra special control training on your dog. When you take your dog to the field for a workout, he should be "heeled" to the place where you will turn him loose to start the workout. Now you will give the command "whoa." Sometimes a young dog, or even an older one, will become anxious to get started in the workout and be a little jumpy waiting for you to tap him on the head to send him off hunting. Maybe he will break before you tell him. Here you can easily teach him to wait on two commands before he breaks out. He must wait for you to tap him on the head and also to say "all right" before he goes.

You have him at "whoa" and have a checkline fastened to his collar. Have about two feet of slack line between you and the dog. Now just tap the dog on the head without saying anything to him. He will make a wild break to go hunting but will hit the checkline, and you will bring him back at once and put him at "whoa." Then you will tap him gently on the head which will probably send him out into the checkline again which will no doubt up-end him, and you will bring him back at

45

"whoa." Repeat this until he stands, even though you tap him on the head. Then when he stands at "whoa" tap him on the head and say "all right." You may have to break out with him a time or two to get him started, but do this training every day, and it will be only three or four days until you can't start him until you tap him on the head and say the word "all right." He will understand the combination that starts him.

This is your yard work that will make it easy for you to do a good job of training. Until your dog is completely finished on handling birds in his training, the yard work should be given every day if possible. Later on, one can give the yard work two or three times a week, enough to keep the dog sharp and to enjoy the association with you.

CHAPTER VI
The Force Method
Of Retriever Training

Many dogs are excellent natural retrievers and do it promptly and tenderly from the first bird they see shot down until their last hunt when old age will not let them go afield anymore. But suppose your good natural retriever decides he will not retrieve any more birds, or instead of that, suppose he decides to eat the birds or chew them so badly that they are worthless. The dog that is hard mouthed should be punished for this, but it may be that a little punishment will make him ignore the downed bird. You may have no way of making him retrieve for you unless he is a force trained retriever.

Some dogs as they grow older have a tendency to become hard mouthed, especially the dogs that are used for pheasant hunting. A crippled pheasant can give a dog a rough time by beating its wings against his head and face and clawing him. The bold dogs soon learn that by chewing them the punishment from the pheasant stops. The tenderhearted dogs just refuse to have anything to do with the bird after a beating or two from a pheasant. If you have a crippled running pheasant you may have to do the retrieving, so as a good conservationist you need a good force trained retriever. I believe that all bird dogs and all members of the retriever breeds should be force trained retrievers.

A retriever trainer once brought me a labrador that did all that was required of him to win trials except retrieve tenderly. He could really chew up a pheasant on his way in to the handler. After he was force trained he did his share of winning, by doing his retrieving the way it should be done. Like all phases of bird dog training, there is a proper time for this training and the stage must be set. My experience over the years has been that if a dog has been force trained before any field work has been given, he may want to do nothing but retrieve. Then too, you can find out if he is worth training. It would be good to work him on wild birds so that he learns to get out and hunt and know what he is hunting. After some hunting experience one can then work him on pigeons a few days. Build up his boldness by killing a few pigeons for him before starting his force retrieving course. After he has been shot over for a week or two, whether he is a good retriever, hard mouth, or will have nothing to do with a shot bird, I discontinue the field work until I have him force broken to do a perfect job of retrieving before taking him back to the field to put the polish on his work.

To say just how long it takes to force train a dog is just a guess since each dog is different in how long it takes to make them happy retrievers. They must be happy in their work, or the job has not been done well. A month might be a good average time considering the easy ones, the not so easy, and the hard ones. The thing you must remember is that your dog must be a prompt, tender retriever to your hand and show you that he is happy to do it for you.

When you are force training a dog to retrieve, you must have his complete and undivided attention. For this work I prepare a room in the barn where there is nothing to distract his attention. What he sees or hears can bother him in his training and will take longer or the job can be a complete failure. In the room that you use, the barer it is the better. There is less for the dog to give his attention to that has nothing to do with the work at hand. After you have started this training, I am sure you will soon see that your dog will give his attention to anything he can until he is far enough along to begin to understand what you are trying to do.

For easier control over the dog, use a swivel harness snap, and nail it to the wall with a fence staple. For an average size pointer or setter nail the snap to the wall about twenty-four inches from the floor. You must have a good strong collar that fits right so that the dog can't slip out of it or break it.

For the first few steps of the training you will need what we call a retriever buck. The best one is a piece of shovel handle, usually made from hickory wood. It should be cut about eight or nine inches long, and the buck should be about two inches in diameter so that the dog will have to open his mouth a little to take it.

Now you are ready to bring the dog into the room for his first lesson. He may come willingly or he may be a little timid the first few times, so take your time and give him time to look around and to smell so that he is satisfied with what he sees and smells. Lead him over to the snap on the wall and snap it to his collar. He may not like this at first, so after you have snapped him to the wall let him stand a few moments or do what he wants. He will soon see that he cannot get loose. Now turn him so that his left side is next to you. If he is still a little jumpy and nervous, pet him and make over him so he will not be afraid. You should drop to your knees so that you are not too tall to work with him.

The word you are teaching now is "fetch." With the buck in your left hand and holding it near your dog's mouth, place your right hand over his muzzle and gently force your thumb between his jaw teeth to open his mouth. Repeating the word "fetch," put the buck in his mouth. Quickly put your left hand under his jaw and with your right hand take hold of the hide on the back of his neck to steady him. All the time that you are doing this repeat the word "fetch." Usually the first few times the dog will throw the buck out of his mouth. You must not punish or hurt the dog at this time or you will lose time. You must help him all you can several times. It is no time to lose your temper. Just start over again and each time you must repeat the word "fetch," as well as repeat the word "fetch" while he is holding it. A person may feel as though he should say "hold it," but one word at a time for the dog to learn is enough right now. "Hold it" will come in a few days.

After a few times of putting the buck in his mouth as you repeat the word "fetch" he will begin to hold it better. Let him hold it five or ten seconds. Should he try to spit it out, tap him under the jaw with your left hand. You must not be rough or brutal here at this stage of teaching. When he does hold it for a few seconds, take it from him and pet him and make over him, stroking him under the jaw. Let him know you are pleased, after which you and the dog rest for a few moments. Twelve or fifteen minutes is long enough for man and dog.

It will be good to repeat the first day's lesson two or three more days. He will learn more solidly the word "fetch," and the better you drill the first few lessons the quicker he will understand what it's all about. It is the foundation of the force training that comes in the next step. After you have worked your dog two or three days on just putting the buck in the dog's mouth, and using the word "fetch," reach down with your right hand and pick up the dog's left forefoot. You are holding the buck in the position to his mouth. Squeeze hard enough to either make him cry out or try to bite you. At the same time repeat the command "fetch." As he opens his mouth put the buck in his mouth and let loose of his foot. Stroke him under the jaw and make him hold it for a few seconds and then take it from him. Then repeat this procedure several times, each time making over him when he takes it and holds it. Always use the one word "fetch" when using the force. Some dogs become excited and upset when the force is applied the first few times. If you didn't have them fastened to the wall, it would be difficult to do much with them. As in all parts of training, it's the over and over again that trains the dog.

One of the very important things to remember when you are applying the force by squeezing the dog's foot is that you must never twist the dog's foot or leg in trying to get him to open his mouth. The small bones in his foot and leg can break very easily. After a few applicatons of the force, the dog will

50

reach to grab for the buck at the word "fetch" or as you reach for his foot. You should always take hold of the dog's foot before holding the buck in the position to take it. Doing this he will know what is coming. If you have hold of his foot, he is less apt to refuse to take the buck. As you work the dog the first few times, you may wish you had three or four hands, as he will try every way he can think of to get loose or to not do what you want him to. But your patience of doing it over and over will pay off. Whenever you see a little improvement in his work, make over him and pet him. At the end of each session before unsnapping him from the hook on the wall, take a few moments to pet and make friends with him. It is up to you to keep him as happy as possible during these first few days of retriever training. A scared or abused dog doesn't learn. These first few days of training are the hardest part for the dog to understand, and it is very important that the groundwork is well laid.

After a day or two of the force application, you will notice that your dog is taking the buck better each time even though he may try to spit it out. As soon as he takes the buck, put your left hand under his jaws, and if he tries to drop it tap him under the jaw and repeat the word "hold." See that he holds it a little longer each time. Use the word "hold" now after he takes it, thus introducing the new word "hold."

If he should suddenly drop the buck, you must quickly take the foot and squeeze it and say "fetch, fetch." Most dogs will give it one more try at dropping the buck, but the prompt application of force on his foot will let him know what to expect when he drops the buck.

After a few days he should be taking the buck quickly at the command "fetch," taking it and holding it. Now each time that he takes the buck, when you take it from him give the new command, "let go." This will probably be the easiest command you will ever teach.

The next step is to hold it eight or ten inches away from his mouth to make him reach for it. When he is doing this well, hold it up a few inches to make him reach up for it.

All of this time you are using your left hand to hold the

buck for the dog, and you have hold of his paw with your right hand, ready to apply force should he be slow or refuse to take the buck. Never forget to praise and make over him for each good piece of work. He may not be too happy at this stage of training, but praise and petting will make him happy as the training continues. When you have him doing a good job at this point, it is time to try him without the pressure. Hold the buck before him and say "fetch." He should take it quickly. If he doesn't, continue the force a few more days.

Usually after a few day's training using the force method, the dog's foot will become a little sore and it won't need much pressure on it. If he will now take the buck quickly and hold it, continue this work a few days longer and by making over him he will be showing signs of understanding and will become more happy with the whole proceeding.

The next step is to take him off the snap on the wall. Now using a short leash about three feet long, move him a few feet from where he has been working. Now holding the leash up close to where it is attached to the collar and the buck in your left hand, six or eight inches from his mouth, give the command "fetch." If he doesn't respond quickly, touch his foot. Now he should be made to take a few steps to take the buck from your hand. Then a little at a time, hold it closer to the floor for him.

As soon as his work up to now is good you can change to the buck with the legs on it. When you change bucks always be sure they are clean. Now hold it close to him and give the command "fetch." This buck is new to him so let him smell it and examine it. Should he not grab for it on the command, quickly apply force. He will need it but once if the prior lessons have been done well. Now hold it close to the floor and tell him "fetch." Each time he takes it let him hold it and at the same time praise him. Then the command "let go." Do this several times. Now lay it on the floor directly in front of him with just your forefinger on the buck and give the command "fetch." Repeat this several times so that he is doing it properly. Now try it without your finger on the buck so that he will become used to picking it up without expecting your hand on it. Always point at it when it is on the floor. This will come in handy later when you're in the field and you have a bird down. He will have learned to hunt "dead" where you are pointing. When your dog will take a few steps and pick up the buck and hold it, then step back a step or two so that he has to walk to you to deliver it. Make over him each time he does it. If he is happy at this stage, he is ready now for you ɩo toss it out a foot or so. When he does it well, increase the distance he must go after it and bring it to you.

One should remember that each new step in the training should be done over and over. It may take a few days on each step to get him to doing it right and happily. Never forget to praise and make over him when the job is done right. Anytime he is slow or refuses, be quick to touch his foot or apply the force.

When you have him going out ten or twenty feet and bringing the buck to you, you can now take him out in the yard where there are things to distract his attention from you and the training. Proceed the same as when you were working in the room where you started. Start by handing the buck to him. Then make him reach, then keep it near to the ground, then throw it short distances. When his work is good on the buck in the yard, then it's time to introduce him to the dead bird. For this work I like to use a dead pigeon. Use one that has not been shot up too badly. Many dogs that will quickly take a game bird in their mouths will refuse when first commanded to take a pigeon. If so you will need to use force several times when starting the dog on a dead pigeon. When you have him trained to retrieve a dead pigeon properly, he is well on his way to being a good force trained retriever.

For this part of the training, put a rubber band around the body of the bird to hold his wings close to his body. Remember, one must make it as easy for the dog as possible at the start of all parts of training. Like with a show you must set the stage. Put the dog on the snap on the wall. Then do the same as you did when you introduced the buck the first time. Open the dog's mouth. The dog may accept it readily, and he may spit it out so

When your dog grabs for the bird, let him hold it for a short time while you stroke him under the jaw and make over him.

you must be alert to make him hold it. After you have done this several times and he is holding it properly, then take his foot in your right hand. Holding the pigeon in your left say "fetch" and squeeze on his foot until he opens his mouth to take the bird. At the same time, let up on the pressure on his foot.

If he is eager to take the bird, make over him. If he refuses you must use force. Keep this work up until he is reaching out and taking the bird, high or low without having to use force.

Never forget to praise him for a good piece of work. Now he is ready for you to take off the snap and work in the room. At first work with just short distances, then roll the bird out a little farther. Always when he starts to you with the bird step back a step or two. It will help draw him to you without pulling on the short line you have on him. When he picks the bird up he should come straight to you. If not, draw him to you promptly with the line. Then make over him. Keep this work up until he bounces out to get the bird and brings it to you happily.

Now it is time to take him out into the yard for more of this same work. Use a twenty foot checkline for the outdoor work. Take him to a quiet place where there are no other dogs around to get your student's attention. Have the dog on your right side holding the checkline with your right hand, and hold the pigeon in your left hand. Be sure you have the dog's attention and that he is looking at you as you toss the bird out four or five feet and say "fetch." He should break out quickly as the bird is thrown. If not, touch him on his left front foot with your right foot to let him know the force will come if he doesn't break out after the bird.

If he should refuse to pick up the bird, take him to where the bird is right in front of him. Reach down and grasp his left front foot and with your left hand stretch the rope out toward the bird, squeeze the foot and give the command "fetch." When he grabs the bird, let up on the force and have him hold the bird for a short time while stroking him under the jaw and making over him.

When you have him retrieving promptly in the yard, then it is time to take him to the field to finish the job using a bird killed for him. Some dogs go from the yard and are perfect when shot over in the field. Others may need to be forced a few times. It is seldom they do not retrieve in the field if the work up to now has been done right. One thing that does happen sometimes in the excitement of killing a bird in front of the dog is that he may run to the bird, pick it up, and crush it or chew it. This you must be on the lookout for. If you see that he is damaging the bird, take it from him and throw it out four or five feet. As he grabs it you must get to him and put your left hand over his muzzle and firmly push his lips back and forth against his teeth repeating "careful, careful." Then hold the bird out for him to take, and as he grabs for it say "careful, careful." He will learn the word "careful" very quickly if when you rub his lips against his teeth it hurts. Each time he goes to retrieve, whether it's a fresh shot bird or one you are using to throw out for retrieving, caution him just as he reaches for it. If he doesn't mind the word "careful," the punishment must be given.

Work him every day on one bird shot for him, throwing it out four or five times for retrieving practice. If he isn't coming straight in to you, quickly jerk him to you with the checkline until he does. For several days use a fresh killed bird for retrieving practice in the yard, always watching that he is retrieving promptly and tenderly.

If you want to add a little extra fancy work to your retrieving, you can teach him to retrieve by the head and head only. It takes a little time, but the dog can learn it and is then a more highly educated dog. When your dog is doing a good job of retrieving the buck in the yard, he is ready to teach head only retrieving. For this work I have used a croquet ball. The ball of course he cannot pick up as it is or hold in his mouth. Take a piece of canvas and cut it about two inches wide by ten inches long. Roll this and tack it to the croquet ball so that there is a pad there for the dog to grab. This tab should be about three inches by two. This will give the dog something to take hold of and carry the ball. You must have him well trained on the buck so that he is happy to retrieve for you. Now take him into your training room and roll the ball out a little way and tell him "fetch." The first few times he will try hard to pick up the ball. You should be near his head, pointing at the ball. You can help him some by touching the ball and rolling it over so the tab is easy for him to take hold of. He will soon learn to roll the ball over to get at the tab.

When you have this part of the training well done, it is time to start him on the pigeon. This time leave the rubber band off the pigeon. Hold the pigeon in your left hand with the pigeon's neck and head between your middle finger and forefinger. Your hand covers the rest of the bird's body so there is nothing but the head for the dog to take hold of. Give the command "fetch." If he is bothered by seeing your hand over the bird, take your time on this. After a few times he will become used to looking for the head. When he takes the head into his mouth, command "hold" and let him hold it a little while. When he is doing this as it should be done, take him off the snap and to the middle of the room and work him until he is taking it from directly in front of his mouth. Then hold it a little higher, then a little lower, then out a few inches so that he will have to reach out for it. When he is taking it properly, next lay the pigeon on the floor, covering it enough with your hand so that he must reach for the head, then step back and let him bring it to you. Always keep in mind that he is never ready for the next step in any part of training until you have him doing properly the present step.

Now you can toss the bird out a few feet. As the dog goes to the bird, watch closely and if he starts to pick up the bird by the body give a little jerk on your checkline and go to him and point to the head. It may be that you will need to cover the bird during a few more workouts with your hand so that he reaches for the head only. In the field when the first few birds are shot for him, have hold of the checkline a few feet back of him and go with him for the retrieve. Here he will be more excited and more apt to take the bird by the body. If he does, proceed as you did in the room by putting your hand over the bird's body so that only the head is available. Lots of practice in the yard with the dead bird will perfect him in this extra step of college training.

After your dog is well trained in the yard and in the field under the gun, take him to the field for the next several workouts where the grass cover is about knee deep. This is to teach your dog to "hunt dead" if he hasn't seen the exact spot where the bird fell. The bird you use for this can be a game bird or a pigeon that you have shot in hunting or in a training

57

session. In my training I have found that it will help the dog's scenting ability to use one type of bird one time such as a pigeon, then the next time use a quail or chukkar or pheasant. It will sharpen up his nose, and you will find that he will use his nose better and will be finding more birds for you.

You should use a twenty to thirty foot checkline for this work. Heel the dog into the field with a bird in your pocket and drop the bird without him seeing you drop it. After you have walked another twenty feet, let the dog have the use of the full length of the checkline and say "dead bird," "dead bird." Work him up wind to where the bird is, repeating "dead bird." When he finds it command "fetch." Make over him greatly when this is done and he finds the bird. The praise is what will make a happy retriever out of him.

Do not overdo this work. Probably six or eight times is enough for each workout. All the time you are working with him to find the dead bird in the grass, keep repeating the words "dead bird," "dead bird." And to help the dog, point to where the bird is. Later in the hunting field when you have a downed bird it will save a lot of time if you can make your dog come in to hunt for the bird where you are pointing. Your dog will soon learn that when you command "dead bird" and point in an area where you think the bird is down, that is where he must "hunt dead" for you. For all of this work set the stage carefully and properly. It will make the training job a lot easier for you and the pupil.

CHAPTER VII
Serious Training

When your dog reaches the age of at least twelve to fifteen months and is well started in the field, is hunting nicely, and is starting to flash point some, he is ready for serious training. He should now be well along in his yard training and obeying your commands promptly and willingly.

He will now be trained to be staunch when he points birds and to stay when you flush the birds and kill one or more. He will also be trained to wait until you send him out to make a prompt and tender retrieve to your hand.

For this training he should have his regular yard training every day along with daily workouts in force retrieving. If you have not already force trained your dog to retrieve, it should be done now before any more field work is given. The reason for not field working the dog until force trained to retrieve is that if he does not retrieve properly there is nothing you can do about it. That is the advantage you have with a force trained retriever. Should your dog refuse to retrieve properly you can force him. If the dog is a natural retriever but still refuses to retrieve, there is nothing you can do about it. If you should decide not to force train your dog to retrieve, then you can start the field work and hope for a good natural retriever.

This is probably the most interesting part of training for man and dog, so each day's work in the field should be well thought out. Give careful instructions to a helper who should know to do nothing but follow them exactly. You should be advised that there are some dogs that will not point the first few birds they are worked on. Some will and some won't. Don't worry about this or be in a rush. Keep working the dog every day on a bird or two, and the pointing will come. I have had dogs in training that didn't point for three weeks and then one day they started pointing and trained out easily from then on. One dog that I had never did point pigeons, but I kept working him every day, killing a bird for him daily, and made him steady to shot at the kill. That fall when I started working him on wild birds he pointed them and was a completely polished shooting dog.

Some have said that a dog should only be worked a short time on planted birds or the dog would lose interest. This is not true. A dog can be worked on them a lifetime, and if done as it should be he will like it better every day. What usually causes a dog to lose interest is a mistake made by his trainer. A person decides to train his dog, goes out and buys half a dozen pigeons, and tries to make those six birds last the entire training period.

To keep a dog's interest, you must kill the birds for the dog and let him hunt dead for them and get his mouth on them. After all, if you don't kill birds for the dog, what is in it for the dog? If the dog goes day after day and sees the birds fly away, never getting his mouth on them, one surely can't blame the dog for not being thrilled with the work. Some of the great field trial winning dogs that I thoroughly trained on pigeons, and then turned over to either their amateur owner-handlers or to professional field trial handlers were ten times champion Flush's Country Squire, ten times champion Seairup, triple champion Titanup, champion Zev's Mohawk Skyhigh, and champion Tyson's Elation, and many, many more. These dogs were all trained to be high class hunting dogs. It took several months to train and polish these performers, and if birds had not been shot regularly for them in their training they would have soon lost interest and would never have been the great winning dogs that they were.

Attach the forty foot checkline to the dog's collar. Walk

Seairup, ten time champion.

Tyson's Elation, two time champion.

Greenwood Bill, Jr., many time winner trained on pigeons.

Zev's Mohawk Skyhigh, grouse champion.

the dog at "heel" a short distance out into the field. Then put him at "whoa". He must stand at "whoa" while you walk around the dog, testing to see whether he will obey the "whoa" command when he is excited to go hunting. Always have the checkline where you can get it should he make a break. If he does break, stop him or go after him, take him back, and make him stand a short time. Make him stand at "whoa" until the tap on the head and the command "all right" are given. Never allow any halfway obeying of commands. Let him cast about in his hunting, and each time that he runs into the end of the checkline give a sharp blast once on the whistle. This will get him to paying some attention to the whistle, and later when he is hunting without the checkline on his collar you can blow the whistle to get his attention to come in or change directions of his hunting. You should plan your trip with the dog so that you will be working in a large circle using up about ten minutes. That will be long enough to get the excitable wire edge worn off him before bringing him up to the bird. The field that you are working in should be somewhat open so that you don't get tangled up with the checkline.

Your helper will be planting the bird after you have been out six or eight minutes and then will get back to the truck and out of sight of the dog. You have checked the breeze so that now you will be coming into the breeze which will be blowing over the planted bird. This will give the dog some help in scenting. As you approach the place where the bird is planted, try to get your dog to cast back and forth across in front of you. This will be better than allowing him to pull straight up to where the bird is planted. By casting back and forth the sudden surprise of bird scent will help the dog snap into point, whereas a dog pulling hard may be slower to point. When the dog points, work on up closer to the dog on the checkline so that the dog is close enough to you that you can gently put your hand on the dog's back. This is his first day to point so be gentle. Your helper should be coming up to flush the bird as you put your hand on the dog's back. He should not hesitate here, but walk to the bird, roll it out to flush, and kill it as it flies away. It may be that some dogs do not want to be touched or handled while on point. If the dog shows this, do not put your hand on him. It may be that six or eight birds later he will allow it. Most dogs like to have you handle them on point.

After your assistant has flushed the bird and killed it, he should step back out of your way so that you can work with the dog on retrieving. Throw the bird out into grass and let the dog break out to retrieve it three or four times. This will help him learn to use his nose and provides good practice on his prompt and tender retriever work. Three or four times is enough. Always try to keep the student anxious. He will remember tomorrow what he did today. If there is a breeze, try to work the dog upwind to give his nose some help in the finding of the dead bird. After his retrieving work, water him and put him on the chain and work another dog. Each day there will be a few new things added to your work on the dog.

When I am working a dog that is new at pointing and work in the field, I do not want any talking or visiting with the helper. Many things can distract the dog's mind from the work at a very

While waiting for your helper to flush the bird, work up the checkline, and put your hand on the dog's back and stroke him a few times.

important time. Your helper should know from what you have told him the things he is to do. A word or nod of the head should tell the helper what to do.

The next four or five days when the point is made, work up the checkline and put your hand on the dog's back and stroke him a few times. Your helper has been given the signal to come flush the bird, so the handling can be done while he is coming. The helper needn't run but should come straight to flush and kill the bird. Always allow the dog to break at the shot for the retrieve. The steadying to shot at the kill will come a little later. In fact, the dog will tell you when the time has come to be steadied.

After he has been worked several days in this fashion with birds killed for him each day, you can now start to let him stand a little longer on point before the helper comes out to flush and shoot. The helper should understand this and watch you closely for the signal to come in to flush.

When the dog points, work your way up to him and have hold of the checkline eighteen or twenty inches from his collar. Let him stand on point a bit, and should he make a jump to flush give a little but sharp jerk and speak the word "whoa."

65

Each day the dog should become more bold and better able to understand what you are working at. At this time you can start the work of making him staunch on point. Usually dogs that are new in training may point for a short time and then try to make a jump in to catch or flush the bird. This is why using planted birds works better than relying on wild birds that would flush too easily.

When the dog points, you will work your way up to him and have hold of the checkline eighteen or twenty inches from his collar. Let him stand on point a little bit, and should he make a jump to flush give a little but sharp jerk and speak the word "whoa." When you speak to the dog, speak rather quietly. Don't give the dog the idea that he needs to be shouted at. Little jerks and the "whoa" if he wants to move in should be enough. Have him stand there a moment after being corrected. Do not be rough with him here. Keep all the style and boldness in him.

The next step in staunching the dog on point is to be able

When your dog makes the point, work your way up the checkline so that you are standing even with his shoulders with the checkline in your right hand, if you are on the right side of the dog.

to walk past him out to where the bird is. In most cases with young dogs, as you walk past his head he will then make the real jump to go with you to the bird. This is called "helping to flush" and is certainly not wanted in well trained shooting or field trial dogs. When your dog makes the point, work your way up the checkline so that you are standing even with his shoulders with the checkline in your right hand if you are standing on the dog's right side. Do not have the checkline tight but have very little slack in the line. After you have stroked his back a time or two, start to take a step past the dog. Take just one step and then step back. If he wants to go in with you, give the little jerks and give the "whoa" command. Repeat this two or three times, and then give the helper the signal to come on in for the flush and shot. Do this each day until he will allow you to make the step past him and then back again without trying to go in with you.

When you have the one step made without the dog moving, then try two steps out and then back. In a few days he

When you have made one step without the dog moving, try two steps out and then back.

should be staunch so that you can walk out around where the bird is without the dog trying to help. Now you can arrange with the helper to come out and stand a few yards away to see if the dog will let you walk out and flush the bird. Always keep an eye on the dog. Should he make a break as you kick around as though to flush the bird take him back and make him stand a minute or two. When your dog will stand and let you go out and flush the bird, he is now telling you that it is time to stop this shot breaking. He will now stand there as your helper kills the bird and wait until you give him the command to fetch the bird to you.

For this work go about your training as usual. When the dog points, go to him and lift him and stroke his back a few times. Let him stand on point a little longer each day. Then walk past him, then back, then past him and walk out around as though you were going to flush the bird. He should be staunch for this work. He has watched you walk past him and out to where the bird is so he should not be wanting to jump in or help. Now the dog is ready for stopping of the shot breaking. Gather up the checkline in loops and drop it in front of you as you stand beside the dog. You are to have a good hold on the end of the line; it is better to loop it once around your hand, gripping it tightly. You will have between thirty-five and forty feet of checkline ready for the dog to run out full length and hit the end of the line. If you watch the line closely as the dog is running, you can give a good hard jerk back in the line just as he hits the end of it. The harder he hits the end of the line the quicker he will quit breaking shot.

Now that you have the rope all set, have the helper walk in, flush the bird, and kill it. As the dog breaks out do not speak to him in any way. When he hits the end of the line, go to him at once and bring him back and set up at "whoa." Make him stand a minute or two and stroke his back and repeat the command "whoa" a time or two. After he has stood, then let him go make the retrieve. Work him in this way two or three days. Now work him up for the point as usual. Have the helper flush and kill the bird. You will throw him if he breaks. Then bring him back to stand at "whoa." While you are bringing him back to stand at "whoa," the helper will go out and get the bird and stand eight or ten feet in front of the dog. Let the dog see that the helper has the bird. The helper will throw the bird out, and you can throw the dog as he runs into the end of the checkline. Bring him back and do this performance a time or two more. Do this each day until he does not break out when the bird is thrown. The next step is for the helper to fire the shotgun as he throws the bird out. If he breaks, bring him back and repeat. Most dogs are "rock steady" after four or five days of this work. This work killing birds and demanding the dog to be steady to the shot at the kill, should be kept going now every day. The dog will not lose interest in this work even though it may seem hard on him. The secret of course is the fact that you are killing birds for him, and when he does his job right he gets to make the retrieve. That's the dog's paycheck.

After the dog seems to understand that he is to stand at the shot and kill, he will probably try another time to make the break. This is not the time to lose your temper. Just correct him as though you expected him to break. The really good ones have enough fire and desire for the bird to try it once more. From now on though if you have done your work as it should be and keep it up regularly, he will be "rock steady" the rest of his life.

CHAPTER VIII
Teaching The Dog To Honor The Bracemate's Point

Backing is the honoring of a bracemate's point. It means that the dog that has not found birds but sees his bracemate pointing refrains from flushing the birds. The backing dog suspends hunting until after the handler of the dogs comes to the point and flushes the birds, fires his gun, and kills one or more birds. The backing dog should stand still until the dead birds have been retrieved. Then the handler should go to the pointing dog and send him on hunting, and then to the backing dog and send him on with the hunt.

Some dogs will honor a bracemate's point as far as they can see. In flat country it could be a hundred or two hundred yards, which is much too far and not needed. As mentioned before, the reason for backing is so that the birds in front of the pointing dog are not flushed. One handler cannot handle two dogs properly that far apart. In a case where the dog backs too far away he should be called or brought up to back at a reasonable distance, which could be ten to forty feet.

Many dogs that have been hunted together a good bit learn each other's ways and will honor each other's points as naturally as the act of pointing. Many young dogs will honor a bracemate's point the first time it ever sees any dog on point. Unfortunately there are dogs that won't back, or honor, and must be trained to back, or honor. Some dogs when they see a

70

dog on point will make a run for the dog on point and never slow up until they have flushed the birds, which of course ruins any chance the handler had of getting a shot. Some dogs will come up to a pointing dog very carefully and creep on past the pointing dog until they themselves scent the birds. This is stealing a point. The most difficult one is the dog that sees the pointing dog but darts away as though he had never seen the dog on point.

Sometimes a dog can teach another dog something that a trainer has had great difficulty getting across. Several years ago when I was working an Irish Setter I had most of the training done on the dog except backing, and after many workouts I didn't seem to be gaining on this red dog. I used a thirty-five foot checkline so that if I saw his bracemate point I could catch him and bring him up to back. When I would have hold of the checkline, he seemed to be getting the idea. But if he was running where I couldn't get to him, he would go past the pointing dog and flush the birds. On this day I was using an old

When hunting with a bracemate, the dog that has not found birds but sees his bracemate pointing should refrain from flushing the birds himself; this is called backing.

pointer to find birds. He wasn't overly friendly to other male dogs but could always find plenty of birds, and I knew I needed plenty of backing opportunities for the red dog. After we had been hunting a short time, the pointer was on point. I looked over to see where the red dog was so that I could make a run to catch his checkline. Red had spotted the pointer and was making his move to flush the birds. Red was too fast for me and went past the pointer and flushed the birds. It may have been that the old pointer knew what was coming because even though he had been trained to stop at the flush, on this day he made for Red and a real fight was on. I had a hard time stopping this fight, but since Red was wearing a checkline I tied him to a tree and so then could get the pointer to let go of Red's leg. I got the pointer started off hunting again, and it was just a few minutes until he was pointing one of the singles. I turned Red loose because I wanted to see what he would do this time. When he saw the pointer on point he stopped instantly. I worked the red dog many times after that and with different dogs and never did I see him fail to honor another dog's point after the lesson

These puppies, restrained by a thirty-five foot checkline, are learning to back a pointing dog.

As you approach the pointing dog, be alert so that you notice at once when your checkline dog sees the other dog pointing. This is your signal to speak sharply the dog's name and "whoa."

that the old pointer gave him.

Any dog that has backing troubles should be trained to do it right. The dog should be well yard trained, taught to obey the "whoa" command, and to come promptly when called; this basic training is necessary if the dog is to learn to honor his bracemate's point.

To train the dog that sees a dog on point and makes a run for it to flush the birds, use a thirty-five foot checkline on his collar. This will give you a little help in getting hold of him when you see his bracemate pointing. If you don't want to let him run loose, you can have him "heel," and then when you see the bracemate point, work your dog up toward the pointing dog. As you approach the pointing dog, be alert to when you first notice your dog on the checkline seeing the dog pointing. This is your signal to speak sharply the dog's name and "whoa." Sharp jerks on the checkline will help. You can use pigeons for this work as it will save hours of time trying to find wild birds. Then too the perfect control that you have with the checkline is an advantage. You should have a helper for this. You will need a well trained dog to do the pointing. Have the helper dizzy a pigeon and put it in a good place in the field where the backing dog can see the pointing dog at some distance. Then the helper should take the dog that is to point and work it around to where it makes the point. At the same time you will take the backing dog with the thirty-five foot checkline on a hunt in a different direction. When you see the pointing dog on point, work the backing dog toward the pointing dog. As you approach watch when your dog first sees the pointing dog, then speak his name and add sharp jerks on the line if he doesn't stop.

The surprise of seeing a dog on point will cause many dogs to back. Work your way up the checkline so that you are standing beside the dog. Reach down and stroke him gently on his back, then lift him by the tail. Then start to step past him, then step back using much the same procedure as you would if he was on point.

The dog that doesn't appear to see a dog on point should be called to you and made to come up extra close to back.

As with all training, when teaching a dog to back, it's the every day work that gets the job done.

When birds are killed, the backing dog should be asked to retrieve a good deal. Getting birds in the dog's mouth will do a lot of good things for any dog. Like all training, it's the every day work that gets the job done.

CHAPTER IX
Gunshy Dogs And Their Cure

Gunshy dogs and their cure are one of the really interesting things in the field of training hunting dogs. To a dog that is gunshy, the sound of a shotgun being fired is a terrifying experience. A gunshy dog has no way of knowing what the noise is or whether it will hurt him.

The part that I have found so interesting in my training program has been to watch a dog come back from the deep dark depths of the gunshy tomb to become the bold and valuable hunting dog that he was intended to be.

There are two things about gunshys that are certain. They are either gunshy or not gunshy and they are made so by men. Some may feel that being gunshy is inherited; however, this is not true. Certain blood lines may tend to be more nervous, which makes it easier for poor handling to cause a dog to become gunshy. If the proper procedure is followed and care is taken in the introduction of the shotgun, the dog will not be gunshy and will understand that the gun is part of the fun in hunting. Many dogs are thundershy. There is no connection between gunshyness and thundershyness. Thunder does not sound like a shotgun. A dog cannot understand where the noise is coming from and you cannot show him. Thunder shyness usually shows up in older dogs including many dogs that have been shot over for years.

I have cured hundreds of gunshy dogs over the years.

Some were dogs that were to be used for hunting, and some were destined to be field trial dogs. Many times when a gunshy was brought to me for the cure, I would ask the owner how he made him gunshy. One owner took his pup to the trap and skeet field, tied him to the bumper of his car, and left him. The dog was probably a little afraid anyway and leaving him to listen to hundreds of shotgun blasts sent him down the gunshy road. Another owner set a pan of feed down and when the pup started eating, fired his double barrel. Another gunshy was made. One owner said some fire crackers were thrown in the dog's pen. Another took his puppy to the field but didn't see any birds or rabbits for the pup to chase so fired the gun anyway a few times.

Every one of these dogs was man-made gunshy, and it could have been avoided with a little planning to set the stage for this chapter in the dog's life. I have always taken gunshys on a guaranteed basis. If I could not cure the dog, I would not charge anything for my efforts. In a period of fourteen months I cured fifty-one gunshys. Then I missed two straight. On one of the dogs I was in too big a hurry, which is something that dog training has no time for in any department.

Over the years in experiments I have tried introducing the shotgun in different ways including the one where you shoot while the dog is eating and the one where you shoot cap guns. They are a waste of time and caps for your cap gun, and a very poor way to start a dog with a gun. One of the big faults in the cause of gunshys is that we humans try to hurry the dog. The more you hurry a dog in training, the slower the dog learns. This is true in every department of dog training.

My first encounter with a gunshy dog was when I was eleven or twelve years old. I lived in what was known as the Mississippi River Flyway, and duck hunting was good from early fall until spring. At that time we were allowed to use live decoys. My dog was a dead grass Chesapeake Bay Retriever bitch. She was about fourteen months old, and I had worked her all summer on retrieving my hobbled decoys out of a pond and she was perfect in this work, never hurting them. The thing

I didn't know about was starting her with a shotgun. Opening day came and Patsy and I were in a blind about daybreak when several mallards came into my decoys. I opened up with a five shot automatic and had five or six dead and cripples down. I called "fetch" to Patsy but she was nowhere around. After I retrieved the ducks, I started for home and to look for Patsy. She was waiting for me about a half mile from where the shooting had been. Since I had never been around a dog that was afraid of the gun, I still didn't know she was gunshy. We had gone a short distance toward home when a rabbit came out of the brush. I shot the rabbit, and Patsy left again in a big hurry. Then there was no doubt in my mind that she was afraid of the gun. From then on I would tie Patsy to a tree about a hundred and fifty yards from where the shooting would be. When I was through shooting I would go get her and bring her to the river and throw sticks at the dead and crippled ducks, and she would bring them in. Patsy lived to be past eleven, and every duck season that was the way Patsy did her retrieving as a gunshy.

There have been untold numbers of dogs made gunshy through carelessness or the improper introduction of the shotgun. There is no need to waste time and twenty-two bullets or light loads in starting the dog. A bullet whether it is a blank or a live shell makes a sharp report, and as you know there is no resemblance to a twelve gauge shotgun shell. Always be sure your dog has been into game many times and is chasing strongly before ever taking the shotgun to the field with the dog. If the dog should let up in the chase when the gun is fired and show a bit of fear, then you haven't had him chasing enough. Leave the gun at home a while longer. There are a great many dogs made gunshy when the open hunting season is on. A lot of young dogs are taken hunting that have never heard a gun. During the open season is not the right time to start the dog and gun. Too many times a dog may not see what you are shooting at, and if you should walk up a bird this could cause a problem.

In my work as a professional gun dog trainer dogs are sent to me any month of the year, and of course some of these months the season is closed for work on wild birds. One of the very good reasons for using pigeons or game farm birds to train dogs and to cure faults is that we can't work dogs in the field during these closed season months. The wild birds must have some time of not being distrubed so they can raise their young. Then too in the South and in some northern states the snake problem is a real danger. With planted birds one can start the young dog so that he knows what birds are, and one can start him properly with the shotgun. If it is needed he can be cured of gunshyness. Many of the great dogs of the field trial world are dogs that have been cured of gunshyness. One of these dogs was a young three year old pointer sent to me for training. He loved hunting and he loved birds, but when the gun was fired it was all over with him. He cured up in about a month and trained out beautifully on handling game properly. He went out into the field trial world and won three field trial championships. This champion Titanup was owned and handled by Dr. George Oehler, one of the all time great amateur handlers and a member of the Field Trial Hall of Fame.

This champion, Titanup, was owned and handled by Dr. George Oehler, one of the all time great amateur handlers and a member of the Field Trial Hall of Fame.

Some gunshys I have had in to be cured were actually afraid of the sight of a shotgun. To begin to cure dogs that were afraid of the gun I would put a shotgun in the kennel with the dog. Some of the dogs slept outside the kennel away from the gun for several days. After some of the regular gunshy work, the dog soon paid no attention to the shotgun.

Another gunshy brought to me for the cure was a big pointer. I was about at the point of giving up on him for it seemed that he just wasn't going to get over the fear of the gun. Every day he would dig a hole in the ground and try to hide in it, and he showed no gain in his condition. One day after we had finished working one of the dogs I walked past the gunshy carrying the dead pigeon. He made a grab for the dead pigeon so I tossed it to him. He promptly ate it feathers and all. I thought this might be the opening I had been waiting on, so after each dog that we worked I would throw the dead bird to him and he would eat it. We noticed that he was watching and waiting for the bird, and in a few days he was completely cured of gunshyness and, strange as it might seem, he made one of the good, prompt and tender retrievers.

When training normal dogs or when curing a dog of gunshyness or birdshyness, the trainer must watch for any condition or action that might help get the job done. The same thing that might work on one dog may not work on another, but one should be alert and take advantage of anything that will help. An accident happened to me and a young dog that was giving me trouble in getting cured of gunshyness. My pupil was a young pointer that I felt was close to being cured but still wasn't just right with the gun. I was working him on a plantation in Alabama. There were tenant farmers scattered all over this huge farm, and each tenant had the usual farm animals, a mule or two, a cow, a few goats, and a flock of white leghorn chickens. My dog cast over near a tenant's home and saw the white chickens. He went to work on them immediately. I knew then that I was going to pay for some dead chickens so I got my shotgun out of the scabbard, loaded it, and fired twice. The dog paid no attention, and I continued shooting until he had killed six and had put the balance up on the house and into the trees. After I paid an astonished farmer for the slain poultry, I went on hunting and found and killed quail and the dog was completely cured. I had just taken advantage of a situation that hurried the cure of a gunshy.

If you have two or three good bold dogs that are ready for serious training, take the gunshy along to the field and put it on the chain between the two bold dogs. The bold dogs will bark and jump and want to be out where you are working a dog, and they will shake up the shy dog and he sometimes will want to fight the bold dogs. This will get his mind off of the shooting, so do not scold any of the dogs for barking or wanting to fight while on the long chain. Work all of your training dogs, and after each workout take the dead or crippled bird and toss it to the shy dog. If he pays no attention to it, at first don't worry. He will after he has been on the chain a few days.

The gunshy may seem even worse the first few days but pay no attention to him. Don't pet him or make over him. He will figure the whole thing out by comparing himself with the other dogs. When he starts barking and jumping and you see that he is watching what's going on in the field, then you can see that he is nearly cured. Here is the time above all to be very careful. A few more days on the chain won't hurt him and will make him even bolder. Previously he has had the company of the other dogs on the chain whether he liked them or not, so he is bold in their company. If you take him out to work him too soon, he will quickly realize he doesn't have the other dogs for company and may become worried. If he does it could set you back in the cure a little longer. Leave him on the chain a few days longer and be sure.

When you do feel he is ready for a workout, work him the next day first. Have a pigeon planted and work him out to it with the wind to your back. Have the helper get his attention by kicking around some, and then flush the bird and let the dog chase. This day do not have the gun in the field. If he breaks out strongly for the chase, then tomorrow you can shoot the bird. You must never forget that a mistake may set you back several days. After two or three days if he is all right with the one shot, then have the helper use a gun with two shells in it. Fire and kill the bird with the first shot, then shoot once more quickly. If the dog pays no more attention here, he is cured.

CHAPTER X
Bird Shy Dogs

To call a dog a bird shy in nearly all cases is to wrongly describe the dog. The real fear of the dog in regard to the bird is caused by uncertainty about what will happen to him after he has any contact with the bird. Actually he is not afraid of the bird. If he is out hunting himself and knows no one is around to either shoot the gun or whip him for not pointing staunchly, he is just as bold as any dog.

Some dogs have been whipped too much for not handling the game right. The dog then decides he must not get near enough to the game to flush it, so he dodges away from it. When your dog makes this decision, you have what is known as a blinker. He will keep right on hunting merrily but keeps away from game. You may wonder why he never finds game and might think he has a poor nose when in reality he has an extra good nose to keep him out of trouble.

Another blinker is the one that establishes a point, and then as the gunner approaches, circles the birds or goes off hunting and maybe just goes away and watches. Then he may come in to retrieve. Like gunshys, there are no partly bird shys. They are either bird shy and blinkers or not, and their conditions are caused by man. Any dog that blinks has a fear in his heart about something. It may be that he was made a blinker when he was made gunshy. Too many whippings can make a dog decide that it is safer not to find birds. What is cruel treatment to one dog may not bother another dog enough to make a blinker out of him. Sooner or later any dog that gets too much abuse will be cowed and do no job at all. There is a big difference between "breaking" and training a dog.

I have always guaranteed to cure any dog that was gunshy or I would not make any charge for anything. I told the owners that the guarantee was good if the dog was gunshy only and not bird shy. However, more that half the gunshys brought to me were bird shy too.

Many of the owners when they noticed that the dog was gunshy continued taking the gun to the field with the dog, shooting at game thinking they could cure the dog. This in most all cases of gunshyness was the cause of bird shyness, too. The dog soon learned the connection between the gun and the bird; the dog's reasoning told him that if he did not produce something to shoot at, then he would not hear the gun. I was getting so many that were both bird and gunshy that it was necessary to work out a way to cure bird shys along with the gunshys.

In my regular training of bird dogs I use a large amount of pigeons. I have on hand most of the time from three hundred to two thousand birds. I thought that if I could get a dog excited and interested in pigeons that this would take care of the bird shy problem. A greal deal of this work with bird shys is the same as with the gunshys, but not all.

I had several pens of pigeons with two or three hundred pigeons in each pen. I built an escape proof pen between two pigeon pens and put in two bird shy dogs and a bucket of water. An hour later I came back to see what progress I had made. Both dogs were huddled together in one corner of the pen afraid of the pigeons as they flew from one end of the pen to the other. I had a couple of eight or ten months old puppies that were bold as lions so I put them in the pen with the bird shys. The pups didn't bother to look at the two timid dogs but started chasing the pigeons back and forth in the pen and keeping them on the move. I watched this for fifteen or twenty minutes, and still the bird shys were not responding. I then took all the dogs out and back to their pen since the pups had had about all the exercise they could stand for a while. Each day I would put the two pups and the two bird shys in the pen together for twenty or thirty minutes.

After three or four days I noticed that the bird shys were watching the pups and the birds. Each day they grew a little bolder. In another three or four days the shy dogs joined in the chase. The next day I only put one pup in the pen with the shys. They all kept up the chase. The next day I put the shys in the pen alone, and it made no difference. They were not a bit afraid of the birds. After a few more days in the pen, I started taking them to the field where I was working the regular string of dogs. I put them on the long chain where they could see and hear everything that went on. In a couple of weeks they were cured of the bird shyness and bold as lions around the pigeons and quail that I was using.

When working several dogs in training, I put the shy dog in between two good bold dogs. The bold dogs barking and jumping and shaking up the shy dog will soon convey the message that there is nothing to be afraid of. Once the shy dog starts watching out in the field where a dog is being worked and sees the birds shot and retrieved, he wants to be out there joining in the fun.

One thing that a trainer does not want is a mistake that will set a dog back once you have made some gain with him. When one thinks a dog is about cured and ready to be worked in the field, he must be extra careful. It is a good policy to wait another few days. Then the day I decide to start him in the field work, I work the dog first and do not take the gun to the field. Bring him to where the bird is planted with the wind to your back. He is not to scent the bird. The helper can get the dog's attention and then flush the bird and break and chase with the dog. The main point here is to have the dog chase at the flush.

If the dog chases strongly, then in another day or two when you work the dog have the helper take the shotgun with one shell. If the dog breaks out strongly, the helper shall shoot at once and kill the bird.

After the dog has been worked once a day for several days, then use a double barrel or automatic. Shoot once to kill the bird, then shoot quickly again while the dog is running to where the bird fell. He will not hear the second shot because of his desire to get to the bird. The reason for not using the shotgun in the first days' work in the field is that up to now he has been on the chain in the company of the other dogs.

When taken out alone he may sense the difference and start to worry so take one thing at a time with him. Usually a dog that has become bold on the chain is ready to work, but it is best not to take any chances.

If you have a pigeon pen for your supply of pigeons, put the checkline on the dog and take him to the pen where he can see the birds. Give him enough checkline so that he can chase beside the pen. When training dogs that seem afraid or not interested, take them inside the pen. You may not see much improvement the first day or so but like with all dog training the success comes with repetition. Eight or ten minutes is long enough either inside the pen or on the outside. You don't want the dog to become tired of the fun and excitement.

CHAPTER XI
The Gunshy Horse

A gunshy horse is a dangerous animal to a person who trains dogs from horseback. A trainer needs to give his entire attention to his dog that he is working, so a gunshy horse can hurt you when you least expect it.

I've owned a few horses that were gunshy and have been thrown when someone shot a gun. When a horse puts you off his back, he doesn't give you much time to pick a soft spot to fall on. A beautiful mare that I owned put me off a couple times so I decided that I should get her over gunshyness or sell her. She was a top grade dog training horse except for the one fault, and I hated to get rid of her. But as she was, she was worthless to me.

At that time I had four other horses that I could shoot the gun around, and they would pay no attention to the shooting. One evening I decided not to feed any of the horses and see if I could make any headway in getting the mare used to the shotgun. The next morning I put them all in a small corral and put several blocks of hay out for the horses to eat. Since they had not been fed the night before, they went to the hay quickly and started eating. I had put out our long dog training chain nearby and had about twenty dogs to work on pigeons. When the first dog was worked and the shot fired, I looked over at my gunshy mare. She jumped and started running around the corral. The other horses kept on eating as though nothing had happened. Very soon the mare quieted down and began eating again. Then we worked another dog, and the mare repeated her scare. After several dogs had been worked and several shots had been fired, I noticed that she was watching the other horses and coming back to eat quickly. We kept on working dogs and shooting, and before we had worked the entire string of dogs she was not showing near the fear that she had at the start. We kept on working dogs and shooting, and the mare seemed a little less bothered by the shooting. I did notice though that she stayed rather close to the other horses when she was eating. It seemed to be another case of one animal getting the message to another.

Each day I put her in the corral with the other horses to eat hay while we were working the dogs. Each day I put one less of the bold horses in the corral with her. In a few days of course she was alone in the corral and paying no attention to the shotgun shooting. She had heard about a total of a hundred shots. I used her in several seasons of dog work, and she was the perfect dog training horse.

Afterword

Field trials have had a tremendous influence on people by encouraging them to own better bird dogs and to have them more highly trained.

In most of the early field trials, dogs could make many mistakes in handling game and still be considered in the winner's column. Over the years trainers have learned how to do a better job of educating a dog, and in today's trials dogs seldom make a mistake in handling game, yet the exciting fire and class of the dog remains.

It is interesting to compare the field trial dogs of yesteryear with those of today. The dogs of today have far more style than the early field trial contenders. In those days, many of the dogs pointed with the tail level with the back or at ten or eleven o'clock. Today the tails are straight up or nearly so. This of course is because the breeders have selected their brood stock carefully in order to have better bird dogs; dogs with the style we see in the present day shooting dogs and field trial dogs are the result of their planning.

The American Field organization has done a wonderful job in the progress of bird dogs and field trials. The American Field Quail Futurity and the American Field Pheasant Futurity are both under the supervision of the American Field organization.

Then, too, credit goes to the Field Trial Hall of Fame which honors the many individuals who have done so much for the great sport of field trials, as well as honoring the great winning field trial dogs.

Whether they are to be shooting dogs or field trial dogs, all bird dogs need to be well trained.

I hope that this work on dog training will be useful and helpful to anyone who wants to train his own dog.

I have tried to write it fully and explain it as though you were standing in the field with me as I worked the dog in training.

I believe you should read each chapter over several times so that you thoroughly understand each step in training.

INDEX

ABOUT THE AUTHOR

Al Brenneman's introduction to guns, hunting, and hunting dogs came when he was quite young. He was allowed to accompany the older men hunting even when he himself was too young to be trusted with a gun. Instead he was given the job of carrying whatever game was killed, usually ducks and rabbits. He gained much experience from the hunters and especially the dogs, whether they were duck retrievers or rabbit dogs.

Growing up in the Mississippi River flyway, his hunting was from early fall until early spring, shooting ducks in the morning and evening and rabbit hunting through the middle of the day. When he was barely in his teens, someone gave him a bird dog, and from then on his main love became bird dogs and bird hunting. With that start in life it seemed natural to take up professional dog training as a career.

As a professional trainer, Brenneman has trained many dogs that have gone on to become field trial champions on the major circuit and he himself has served as a judge at some of the field trials. As his reputation grew for curing dogs of faults often thought to be incurable, he began his systematic study of successful training techniques. Eventually he himself learned to believe that he could cure practically all bad faults of bird dogs ranging from blinkers to gunshys to bird shys.

Brenneman's long-awaited book records for the first time a life associated with bird dogs that continues to today from his childhood begun along the banks of the Mississippi.

ORDER FORM

BOOK WORLD
P.O. Box 708
Frankewing, TN 38459

Dear Sirs:
   Please send me _____copy(ies) of AL
BRENNEMAN TRAINS BIRD DOGS at $16.45
plus $1.00 for mailing and handling. Enclosed is
my check for $_____ made out payable to
Book World.

(See Other Side For Address Form.)

BOOK WORLD
P.O. Box 708
Frankewing, TN 38459

_____
(NAME)

_____
(ADDRESS)

_____
(CITY)   (STATE)   (ZIP)